Home
SEWING
Techniques

Home
SEWING
Techniques

Essential sewing skills to make
inspirational soft furnishings

Cheryl Owen

IMM lifestyle books™

Read. Learn. Do What You Love.

Originally published by New Holland Publishers (UK) Ltd

Published 2015—IMM Lifestyle Books
www.IMMLifestyleBooks.com

IMM Lifestyle Books are distributed in the UK
by Grantham Book Service.

In North America, IMM Lifestyle Books are distributed by
Fox Chapel Publishing
1970 Broad Street
East Petersburg, PA 17520
www.FoxChapelPublishing.com

ISBN 978-1-5048-0003-7

10 9 8 7 6 5 4 3

Printed in China

Contents

Introduction

Soft furnishings can completely change the look of your home, making it fashionable, comfortable and a joy to live in. You don't need to spend a lot of money or be an accomplished needleworker to attempt most home sewing projects. A few simple items such as a cushion or throw are quick and easy to make, and will give you the confidence to move on to more challenging projects. Making major features such as curtains can save you a serious amount of expense, as well as affording you the opportunity to custom make them to the exact size you need and in the fabric you want.

This book will guide you reassuringly through all the techniques involved in home sewing, each explained in turn with one or more accompanying projects that demonstrate not only the featured method but some of the other key techniques. This means that you will soon become adept at applying the whole range of sewing skills to create fabulous fabric items with ease. Many of the projects would be lovely to make as gifts—a handcrafted present is always extra special and shows you really care. Most of the items use small amounts of fabric, which means you can delve into that stash of enticing fabrics you may already have just waiting for the right home décor idea. But otherwise, there is an amazing choice available to buy nowadays from stores and online. If you are already an enthusiastic needleworker, be bold and use these projects as inspiration to design your own innovative soft furnishing creations.

Getting Started

It is important to check that you have all you need before you embark on your home sewing endeavours. There is nothing more frustrating than finding you are missing a vital piece of equipment or that you don't have enough fabric for a project part the way through, especially if you then discover that your chosen colourway or pattern is no longer available.

When it comes to basic sewing skills, there is more to home sewing than just stitching. Cutting out the fabric is a major part of the process too, and will often give you a sense of how the finished item will look.

Equipment

Even if you are a novice needleworker, you will probably have some basic sewing equipment. Gather these items together and store in one place, using this equipment only on fabrics and trimmings so they don't become dirty and blunt. Work on a clean, flat surface that is well lit—daylight-simulation light bulbs are kind to the eye and won't distort the colour of fabrics and threads. Keep sharp implements out of the reach of young children or pets.

Pattern-making papers

Pattern paper is available from haberdashery (notions) stores; some large department stores will also sell sewing materials and tools. Tracing paper or greaseproof (wax) paper can also be used, and is especially useful when you need to see through the pattern, for example, when positioning motifs.

Pattern-making tools

Draw patterns with a fine pen or a propelling pencil. Draw straight lines against a ruler and describe small circles with a pair of compasses. Use a set square for accurate angles.

Measuring tools

Use a plastic-coated or cloth tape measure to measure curves and to check fabric measurements. A transparent 30 cm (12 in) ruler is a handy size for making patterns and checking measurements. Draw against a metre (yard) stick for long lengths and to measure fabric quantities. A retractable steel measure can be used to measure windows and beds, and is also useful when measuring long lengths of fabric—curtains for example. A 15 cm (6 in) long sewing gauge has a slider that can be set at different measurements for marking hems and seams, and as a guide for quilting.

Pattern-making tools

Rulers and tape measures

Scissors

Cut paper patterns with paper scissors. Bent-handled dressmaking shears are the most accurate and comfortable to use for cutting fabric—the angle of the lower blade allows the fabric to lie flat. Shears are available in different sizes, so test before buying—find a pair that feels comfortable to your hand. The best-quality shears are expensive, but if cared for they will last a lifetime. A small, sharp pair of embroidery scissors are indispensable for snipping fabric and threads. For protection, keep them in a cloth case when not in use.

Fabric markers

Marks made with an air-erasable pen will gradually fade away and those made with a water-soluble pen can be removed with water. Traditional tailor's chalk comes in different colours in wedge and pencil form; the marks will mostly brush off but a slight residue will remain. Always test fabric makers on fabric scraps first. A fine, sharp pencil can be used on fabric, but the marks will stay.

> **Tip:** A good iron and ironing board are essential pieces of sewing equipment. Use a sturdy ironing board. Since you will often be handling large and weighty pieces of fabric, the board must be able to take the strain. Buy the best-quality iron you can afford, ideally a steam/dry iron that has a variable and reliable heat setting.

Scissors

Fabric markers

NEEDLES

Sewing machine needles

These needles come in a range of sizes with different-shaped points, the lower the number the finer the point. Universal needles in size 70–90 (9–14) are the most commonly used. Stitch non-woven fabrics with a ball-point needle. Replace sewing machine needles regularly, as they soon become blunt and put strain on your sewing machine.

Hand sewing needles

In this case, the higher the number the shorter and finer the needle. Sharps needles are long, general-purpose needles—use them for tacking, slipstitching and sewing on buttons. Crewel embroidery needles have a large eye, so are easy to thread with embroidery thread (floss). Mattress needles are very long and are ideal for sewing through cushions, for example, to attach buttons.

Pins

Dressmaking pins come in various thicknesses, but household pins are the most versatile. Lace and bridal pins are particularly fine and will not mark delicate fabrics. Coloured glass-headed pins show up well on a large expanse of fabric such as a curtain.

Bodkin

A bodkin is a needle-like tool with a large eye and a blunt tip. Fasten a bodkin to the end of a rouleau to turn it right side out (see page 77) or to a drawstring to draw it through a channel (see page 85). A safety pin can be used in place of a bodkin.

Rouleau turner

Also called a tube tuner, a rouleau turner has a latch hook to hook onto the end of a rouleau to turn it right side out instead of a bodkin (see page 77). A safety pin can be used instead of a rouleau turner but it will be a slower process.

Bias-binding maker

Draw a bias-cut or straight strip of fabric through this clever metal gadget to turn under the fabric edges, then press in place to make a binding (see page 57). Bias-binding makers come in a range of widths.

Staple gun

Use a staple gun for simple upholstery jobs—it is fast and efficient for attaching fabric to wood (see pages 109 and 114–115). It is a powerful tool so make sure that you don't leave a staple gun where children might play with it.

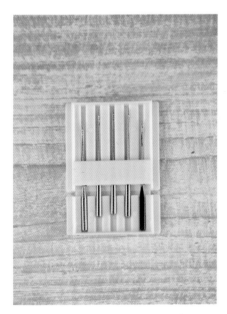

Sewing machine needles

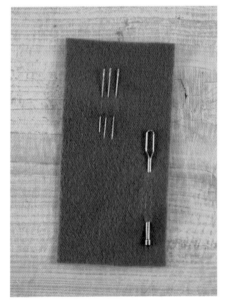

Hand-sewing needles and bodkin

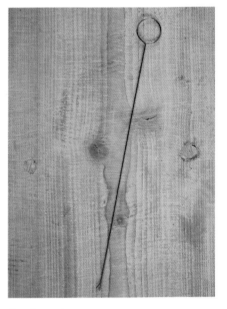

Rouleau turner

SEWING MACHINE

The sewing machine is your best friend when it comes to home sewing. There will always be a place for hand sewing, but stitching by machine saves time and gives a professional finish. There are many factors to consider when choosing a sewing machine because it is the biggest and most important investment for the sewing room. Always buy from a reputable dealer and test-run a few machines to make comparisons in order to see which you prefer. Also ask your friends and family for their recommendations. Check that the machine is simple to thread and that the speed is easy to control. A machine that does straight stitch, zigzag stitch and neat buttonholes will cover most people's needs, but you may fancy experimenting with machine embroidery and there are many exciting models available that offer push-button or computerized controls.

How it works

Although there is a huge range of sewing machines on offer, they are all fairly similar to operate. Read the sewing machine manual to familiarize yourself with the machine's features and operations. Basically, the presser foot holds the fabric in place, while the needle, which is threaded with the upper thread, penetrates the fabric and goes into the bobbin area below to pick up the lower thread in order to form a stitch. This particular machine (below) has a lift-up lid that conceals the spool holder, which holds the reel of upper thread, the bobbin winder, foot pressure dial and the thread tension dial. This is a good design feature, as the lid stops these machine parts getting dusty if the machine is left out. The thread tension dial regulates the tension between the upper and lower thread to form flat, even stitches. The stitches will pucker if the tension is too tight, but if it is too loose, the stitches will also be loose and won't hold the fabric layers together.

Stitch length dial

The numbers on the dial represent either the length of the stitch in millimetres or the number of stitches per inch.

Stitch width dial

Use this dial to set the width of a zigzag stitch. Set it at 0 for straight stitching.

Reverse stitch lever

Lift the reverse stitch lever to stitch backwards. Reverse stitch at the start and finish of a seam to stop the ends of the seam unravelling, or to reinforce a short seam.

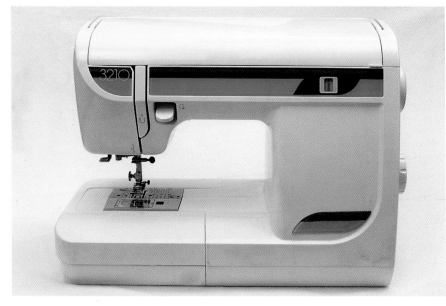

Sewing machine

Machine embroidery thread

Presser feet

Most machines will have a standard presser foot and a few specialist presser feet (see below for the most commonly used by home sewers). There will be a lever to lift the presser foot up and down. The feet can be changed by snapping them on and off or unscrewing and screwing them on.

- **Standard foot** Use for straight stitches and zigzag stitch (this foot will be the main one you will use).
- **Zipper foot** Use when you need to stitch beside a raised surface, such as stitching a zip in place—it can be fitted to the right or left of the needle.
- **Piping foot** Use to stitch in place piping or other raised trimmings such as a pompon trim (or you can use the zipper foot instead).
- **Buttonhole foot** Use for working buttonholes.
- **Overlock foot** Use for zigzag stitching.
- **Blind hem foot** Use for making invisible hems—it ensures that the needle catches only one or two threads.

Needle plate

This metal plate covers the area under the presser foot. The needle enters a slot in the centre of the plate to grab the bobbin thread concealed below. Some needle plates will have a series of lines you can use as seam width guides.

Power supply

For safety, keep the power supply turned off when setting up your machine. Check that the electrical voltage of the machine is the same as your power supply. Plug in the cord socket, then insert the plug into the power supply and switch on the power. Always switch off the machine when it is not in use and pull out the plug from the socket.

Sewing light

Always work in good light. The sewing light on the machine will keep the stitching area well lit and is especially useful when stitching dark colours.

Foot control

Make sure the foot control is placed on a flat floor surface. The harder the foot control is pressed, the faster the machine will run. The sewing speed can be varied on most machines.

Bobbins

Small metal and plastic spools called bobbins are wound with the lower thread and housed underneath the stitching area. When the bobbin thread runs out, it can be refilled and wound on the bobbin winder on top of the machine.

Hand wheel

Once the machine is threaded and the stitch set to the correct length, lift the presser foot and turn the hand wheel to raise the needle. Position your fabric under the needle, then turn the hand wheel to lower the needle until it just touches the fabric. Now lower the presser foot and you are ready to start stitching with the machine.

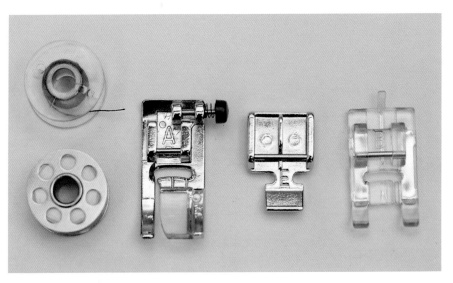

Bobbins and presser feet

Materials

Choosing fabrics for home accessories such as cushions is fun and will give you confidence to tackle more challenging choices such as curtain fabric, which has a large impact on the look of your home.

FABRICS

If embarking on a large project such as curtains, always get samples to view in situ. Look at the fabric in both daylight and electric light, and place it in its intended position. Take care when mixing patterns, as they may coordinate well together but be unsettling to live with on a daily basis. Up-to-the-minute fabrics are inspiring but will date, so limit them to smaller items such as cushions.

Soft furnishing fabric

These fabrics are usually 137 cm (54 in) wide. Check their purpose—some soft furnishing fabrics are suitable for curtains and bedspreads but not for heavy use, such as for chair covers. Soft furnishing fabrics come in many finishes such as chintz—a closely woven cotton—and damask, which features woven surface designs. Some soft furnishing fabrics have the added bonus of a protective stain-resistant finish.

Cotton

Most of the projects in this book are made from cotton, which is a natural fabric that is easy to work with. Cotton is usually inexpensive and comes in various weights and thicknesses. Printed and plain cottons produced with patchwork and quilting in mind are a good choice for beginners. Cotton sheeting is available in very wide widths to make bedding.

Linen

This natural fabric is very strong and drapes well, although it creases easily. Linen blended with polyester is easier to handle but the quality is poorer.

Chenille

This tactile fabric is woven from fringed yarns to give a soft pile. Chenille is not suitable for heavy use, as the pile will wear.

> **Tip:** Plain ready-made chenille throws are inexpensive and can be decorated with embroidery or cut up to make into cushion covers.

Soft furnishing fabric

Cotton fabric

Linen fabric

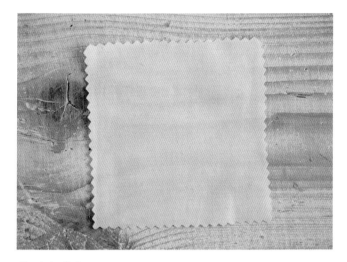

Curtain lining

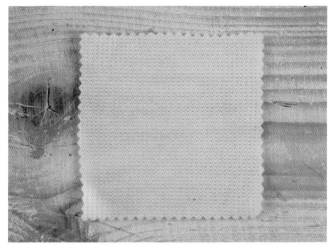

Curtain interlining

Curtain lining

This smooth fabric is available in wide widths to line curtains (see pages 118–121). Choose a natural-coloured lining rather than a distinctive colour, which will fade in sunlight.

Interlining

Interline curtains for heat insulation and to add structure (see page 119). Polyester or cotton interlining is available in a few different weights. Interlining is applied between the curtain and the lining, providing an extra layer of warmth.

Interfacing

Stiffen fabric with interfacing to add extra strength and support. Interfacing is available in different weights and as an iron-on (fusible) or sew-in application. Press the shiny side of iron-on interfacing to the wrong side of the fabric. When pressing, hold the iron in place for a few second then lift and place it in another position and continue. Sliding the iron over the interfacing could make it wrinkle. Tack (baste) sew-in interfacing to the wrong side of the fabric pieces around the outer edges.

- **Medium interfacing** is soft and lightweight; use when you want to add a bit of body to an item.
- **Firm interfacing** is stiffer and will add definition when applied to fabric and pressed-in pleats.
- **Firm flexible interfacing**, as its name suggests, is firm but will still allow movement in the fabric.
- **Iron-on medium-loft fleece** adds soft structure to fabric. Press the fabric to the fleece, as the heat doesn't penetrate the fleece surface easily to fuse it to fabric.

> **Tip:** Don't be nervous about pressing an item that has fleece—it will retain its bounce.

Above: *Curtains hang better if they have been lined*

Wadding   *Tear-away stablizer*

Wadding (batting)

This is most commonly used in quilts, where a layer of wadding (batting) is sandwiched between fabrics to pad them. It comes in various weights, and although it is usually made from man-made fibres such as polyester, you can also find it made from natural fibres such as cotton, wool and eco-friendly bamboo. Keep in mind that cotton wadding and wadding made from other natural fabrics may shrink, whereas those made of polyester won't. If you are planning to wash the item frequently, polyester may be more practical.

Tear-away stabilizer

This non-woven synthetic material is fun to use. Place it under fabric before machine embroidering to add support. After stitching, gently tear away the stabilizer on each side of the stitching. This material is particularly useful when sewing delicate or stretchy fabrics. It stabilizes the fabric and prevents the presser foot from dragging the delicate fabric along and making a mess of the seam. Tear-away stabilizer comes in various weights and can also be purchased in iron-on and adhesive forms.

Above: *Interlining widths can be joined by machine or hand*

Tip: Once stitched, wadding and interlining can be carefully trimmed away in the seam allowance to reduce their bulk.

CURTAIN MATERIALS
Heading tapes

Most curtain headings are created with curtain tape, which is sold by the metre (yard). It has cords running along its length. The tape is sewn to the underside of the curtain at the upper edge and the cords are drawn up to the required widths to gather or pleat the curtain (see pages 126–127).

- **Standard heading tape** produces a simple, gathered heading on a curtain, and works well on informal curtains. It has slots for inserting curtain hooks.
- **Pencil pleat heading tape** gives a neat row of upright pleats. As with standard heading tape, it has slots for curtain hooks.

- **Eyelet heading tape** is designed for using with eyelet rings—the tape has holes cut to use as a guide for cutting holes for the eyelets.

Curtain hooks and runners

Curtain hooks are made from plastic or metal. Slip plastic hooks through the slots on curtain tape and then onto the runners that slot onto the track or attach to curtain rings. Use metal hooks on heavyweight and hand-sewn headings. Some hooks are combined with runners as a single unit. Runners are often supplied with the track. The runners at the outer ends of the track are known as end stops because they literally stop the curtains falling off the end of the track.

Curtain rings

Hang hooks inserted through heading tape onto metal, wooden or plastic curtain rings to hang from a curtain pole. Some curtain rings have a clip attached to clip onto the top of the curtain (see the Café Curtain on pages 94–95). Eyelet rings come in two parts, one for the front and one for the back of the curtain. For best results, use these rings with eyelet heading tape. The rings can be prised apart and removed for laundering the curtains. Allow nine rings per metre (yard) of fabric; you will need an even number of rings, so round up the number of rings to the nearest even number. When hanging the curtains, place the outer ring outside the pole support at either end of the pole.

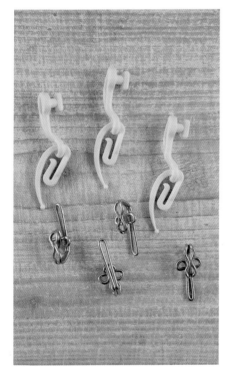

Curtain hooks and runners

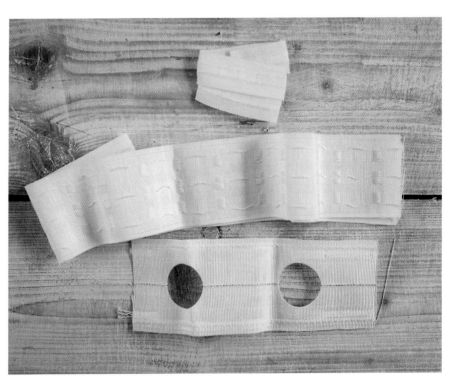

Curtain heading tape

Curtain weights

Most curtains will hang better with weights attached inside the hems. Metal weights are available as discs or as a chain.

THREADS
Sewing threads

Choose a strong, durable sewing thread with some flexibility in it in a colour to match the fabric. Use a general-purpose mercerized cotton thread for woven natural-fibre fabrics and general-purpose polyester thread on woven synthetics and knitted fabrics. Strong polyester thread in a limited range of colours is available for topstitching, making buttonholes and sewing buttons. Use a size 100 (16) needle on your sewing machine when using this thicker thread.

Embroidery threads

Machine embroidery threads have a lovely sheen, and come in a broad range of colours including shaded and metallic. Use them for decorative zigzag stitching. Stranded cotton embroidery thread (floss) is used for embroidery and to make tassels (see pages 134–135). There are masses of exciting embroidery threads and yarns available nowadays, which can be embroidered by hand or couched in place with a machine zigzag stitch or by hand.

BIAS BINDING

This strip of bias-cut fabric has pressed-under edges for binding the raw edges of fabric. Cotton and satin bias binding are available to buy by the metre (yard) or in packs. They come in different widths and colours including patterned fabrics. You can make your own bias binding with a bias binding maker (see page 57).

Curtain weights

Sewing thread

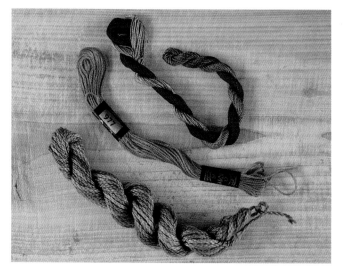

Embroidery threads

Bias binding

PIPING CORD

Cover inexpensive white piping cord with bias-cut strips of fabric to make piping (see pages 60–61) or use the cord as a drawstring (see pages 84–85). It comes in different thicknesses.

TRIMMINGS

Have fun decorating your home sewing projects with the wonderful range of trimmings that are available. Ribbon (see the Ribbon-trimmed Sheet on pages 100–101), ric-rac (see the Towel with Borders on pages 48–49) and pompon edging (see the Round Tablecloth on pages 32–33) are just a few to choose from. Trim your creations with ready-made embroidered motifs, which can either be sewn or fused in place with an iron (see the Oxford Pillowcase on pages 30–31).

Left: *Piping cord*

Below: *Trimmings*

FASTENINGS
Buttons

Buttons come in all sorts of shapes, colours, sizes and materials. Use buttons to fasten cushions and duvet covers (comforters). Flat buttons have flat backs with two or four holes for sewing through, while shank buttons have a loop underneath to sew through. Self-cover buttons come in different sizes to be covered with your choice of fabric, consisting of two parts that fix together (see page 81).

Zips (zippers)

Use zips (zippers) to close two edges of fabric together temporarily, such as on a cushion cover (see pages 72–73). Stitch zips (zippers) with a zipper foot on your sewing machine.

Hook and loop closure tape

This tape comes in two sections, one with a looped mesh surface and the other with a hooked surface, which then interlock when pressed together. The tapes are available in a few colours to sew on or they have an adhesive backing for sticking.

Cotton tape

Utility cotton tape is cheap to buy, and is available in different widths and a limited choice of colours. Use it to make simple ties for soft furnishings.

Buttons

Cotton tape and zips

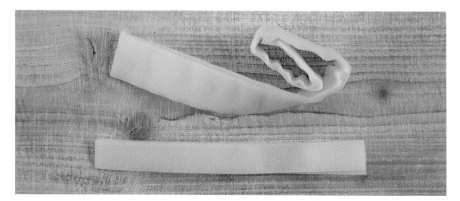

Hook and loop closure tape

PREPARATION AND CUTTING

Although you may be keen to dive in and start cutting your fabric, take your time—cutting is an important part of creating soft furnishings and home accessories, and therefore shouldn't be rushed. Cutting mistakes can be costly and can't be rectified, so make sure you position your patterns with care, accurately and economically. Remember the saying 'measure twice, cut once'. Selvedges (the neatened edges that run the length of the fabric) are often tightly woven and can pucker the fabric, but these can be trimmed off before cutting out the fabric pieces for a smooth finish.

Using patterns

You will find useful patterns and templates on pages 138–141, although many of the projects in this book are simply made from squares and rectangles that can be drawn directly onto the fabric, using a set square and a ruler for accuracy. Draw on fabric with an air-erasable pen, water-soluble pen or tailor's chalk. Sewing patterns have an arrow on them that indicates the grain line. Keep the grain line parallel with the fabric selvedge when positioning the pattern on the fabric. To cut out, lay the fabric flat on a table or on the floor and smooth it out.

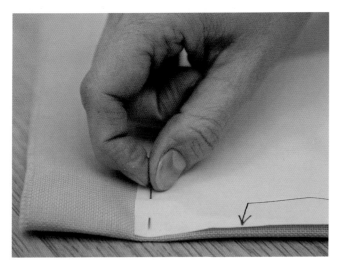

To cut pairs of patterns, fold the fabric lengthways or widthways to make a double layer. Pin the pattern or draw it on top. Patterns where the fabric should be cut to the fold have an arrow with the ends curved towards the fold line—match the fold line to the folded edge of the fabric. Otherwise, keep the fabric single. Mark any dots or crosses on the fabric with a pin, an air-erasable pen or a water-soluble pen, then cut out the pieces. Save any fabric scraps to test stitches and the heat of your iron.

Positioning motifs

If the fabric has a distinctive motif, you may want to show it off, on the centre of a cushion for example. Bear in mind that you may need to buy a larger amount of fabric to allow for positioning motifs. Centre repeat patterns, stripes and checks so that they will be placed symmetrically when the item is made.

Make a pattern from tracing or greaseproof (wax) paper so that you can see through it. Mark on the seam lines and grain line. Fold the pattern into quarters to find the centre, then open out flat again. Lay the pattern over the motif on the fabric, matching the grain lines and centring the motif. Pin in place and cut out.

Matching patterned fabrics

You may need to join entire widths of fabric to make curtains, frills and some other items. If the fabric is patterned, the pattern will need to be matched, and to allow for this you will need to buy extra fabric.

1 Use an air-erasable pen to draw a line across the fabric selvedge to selvedge. Cut along the line. Measure from the cut edge the length required, including allowances such as hems. Cut off the excess fabric. Lay the remaining fabric vertical edge to vertical edge with the first piece, matching the level of the pattern, cut across the fabric to match the first piece.

2 Fold under the seam allowance along one vertical edge. Lay the folded edge over the edge of the other fabric length, matching the pattern. Pin the folded edge to the underlying fabric.

3 Fold over the top fabric, and replace the pins on the wrong side of the fold. Check that the patterns still match, then stitch along the fold with right sides facing. Use a flat felled seam for unlined items and a flat seam for lined curtains (see pages 28–29).

Making a circular pattern

Describe small circles on paper with a sharp pencil and a pair of compasses. If you need a large circular pattern for a round tablecloth or cushion for example, it is simple to make a string and pencil compass to make a quarter circle pattern.

Start with a piece of paper that has two adjacent sides that measure at least the radius of the intended circle. Starting at a corner, measure and then mark the radius on one edge of the paper. Tie a length of fine string to a sharp pencil. Fix a map pin up through the first corner of the paper. Hold the pencil upright on the radius mark and tie the other end of the string to the map pin, keeping the string taut. Draw a quarter circle between the two adjacent edges of the paper. After cutting out the pattern, fold the fabric into quarters, pin the pattern on top, matching the straight edges to the folds, and then pin and cut out.

HAND STITCHES

From time to time, you will need to do some sewing by hand, such as when tacking (basting), closing openings or making hems, and the following stitches are the appropriate ones to use for these tasks.

Tacking (basting)

Join fabric layers together temporarily with tacking (basting) stitches before stitching on the sewing machine. The more you stitch and become confident, the less you will feel the need to tack (baste) seams first, but tacking (basting) is always useful for tricky areas, such as joining many layers of fabric or stitching corners or tight curves.

Tack (baste) by hand or use a long machine stitch in contrast-coloured thread so that the stitches are visible. Generally, sew just inside the seam line to make the tacking (basting) stitches easy to remove, but it is sometimes necessary to tack (baste) along the seam line for accuracy, such as at a corner. Remove the stitches once the seam is stitched unless advised otherwise.

Slipstitch

Use slipstitch to stitch two folded edges together to close a gap or one folded edge to a flat surface to secure bias binding (see page 57) or make a hem (see pages 46–47).

Working from right to left with a single thread, bring the needle out through one folded edge. Pick up a few threads of the fabric on the opposite edge and insert the needle back through the folded edge about 6 mm (¼ in) along from where it emerged. Keep the stitches small and repeat along the length.

Herringbone stitch

Sew lined curtain hems with herringbone stitch (see page 120). Herringbone stitch can also be used decoratively in a larger size—see the Striped Rug on pages 50–53.

Work stitches from left to right, with the needle pointing to the left. Bring the needle out close to the hem edge, make a small stitch in the fabric above the hem about 6 mm–1 cm (¼–⅜ in) to the right, then make a small stitch in the hem the same distance along. Continue to alternate the stitches, spacing them evenly.

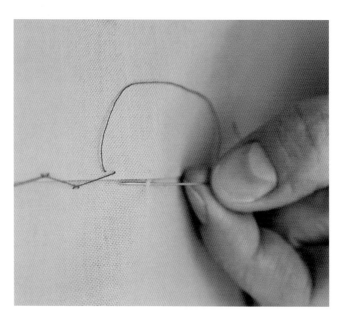

Techniques
and Projects

The techniques described here are needed throughout the home sewing projects. Try those methods that are new to you on scrap fabric before embarking on a project. When following the instructions, it is important to use either metric or imperial measurements, but not a combination of both.

Keep a sewing workbox to hand for all the projects. This should contain dressmaking shears, embroidery scissors, ruler, tape measure, dressmaking pins, sewing threads and needles, a bodkin and an air-erasable pen, water-soluble pen or sharp tailor's chalk. Also make sure you have a fine, sharp pencil, pattern-making paper and paper scissors for making patterns.

Seams

A seam joins two or more layers of fabric together, and the seam allowance is the area between the stitching and the raw edge of the fabric. It is important to keep the seam allowance consistent as you stitch a seam so that the fabric pieces match. The seam line is the imaginary line to stitch along.

Seam Basics

Common seam allowances are 1 cm (⅜ in) and 1.5 cm (⅝ in), and these are used throughout the book. Match the seam allowances and raw edges and then pin together. Either insert pins at right angles to the seam line, as this allows you to stitch over them, or insert them along the seam line pointing towards the start of the seam and remove them as you stitch. See which method you prefer, or it could be a combination of both. If you are new to stitching on a sewing machine or working on an awkward area, tack (baste) the layers together first (see page 24).

Sewing machines have lines on the base plate that are standard seam allowance distances from the needle. When stitching, keep the raw edges aligned with the relevant line to keep the size of the seam allowance constant.

Insert the needle in the seam line about 1 cm (⅜ in) from the start and reverse stitch back to the start, then stitch forward. When you reach the end of the seam, reverse stitch for about 1 cm (⅜ in). These reverse stitches will stop the ends of the seam unravelling. If stitching a continuous seam, such as around a circle, overlap the start of the stitching by about 1 cm (⅜ in). Snip off the excess thread close to the fabric.

> **Tip:** Pressing the item after each seam is stitched helps to achieve a professional finish.

Sewing a Flat Seam

This is the simplest type of seam to stitch and the most frequently used. See the **Neatening Seams technique** on page 36 if you wish to neaten the raw edges of the seam with a zigzag stitch to prevent the raw edges from fraying.

1 With the raw edges level, stitch along the seam line. To turn a corner, stitch to the corner of the seam line and leaving the needle in the fabric, take your foot off the power and lift the presser foot. Pivot the fabric so that the next edge to be stitched is facing you, then lower the presser foot and continue stitching the seam.

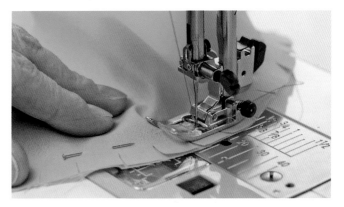

2 When joining a curved edge to a straight edge, snip into the straight seam allowance at regular intervals to help the seam allowance lay flat. Pin or tack (baste) the seam, then stitch in place.

Layering Seams

Reduce the bulk of fabric in a seam allowance by trimming each seam allowance by a different amount after the seam has been stitched.

Always trim the seam allowances of piping as they will be particularly bulky otherwise.

Clipping Corners and Snipping Curves

This helps the seam allowances lay flat and reduces the bulk of the fabric in the seam allowances when the item is turned right side out.

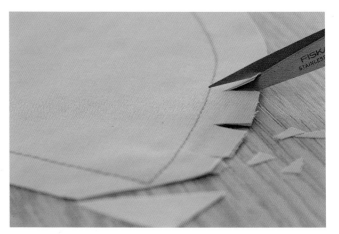

Use embroidery scissors to cut the seam allowance diagonally across a corner, taking care not to cut the stitching. Snip 'V' shapes into a curved seam allowance.

Sewing a Flat Felled Seam

With this type of straight seam, the raw edges are neatly hidden within it. Use on unlined curtains and other items where both sides of the fabric will be visible, for example to make joins in a tablecloth or sheet. Allow a 1.5 cm (⅝ in) seam allowance on flat felled seams.

1 With right sides facing, stitch a flat seam, taking a 1.5 cm (⅝ in) seam allowance. Press the seam in the same direction, then trim the lower seam allowance to 1 cm (⅜ in).

2 Turn under 5 mm (¼ in) on the upper seam allowance, then stitch close to the turned-under edge.

Oxford pillowcase

This kind of pillowcase has a generous flange on all edges, which is stitched after the pillowcase has been made. Outline the flange with an eye-catching gingham ribbon highlighted with a few embroidered motifs available from haberdashery (notion) stores and suppliers. Some motifs are iron-on, while others need to be sewn in place.

1 Press under 1cm (⅜ in) and then 4 cm (1½ in) on one short edge of the back and one long edge of the flap. Stitch close to the inner pressed edges. With right sides facing, pin the back on the front, matching the raw edges.

2 With wrong sides of the back and flap facing up, pin the flap on top, overlapping the hemmed edges and matching the raw edges. Refer to the **Seams techniques** (Sewing a Flat Seam) on page 28 to stitch the outer edges, taking a 1 cm (⅜ in) seam allowance and then clipping the corners. Turn right side out and press the pillowcase flat.

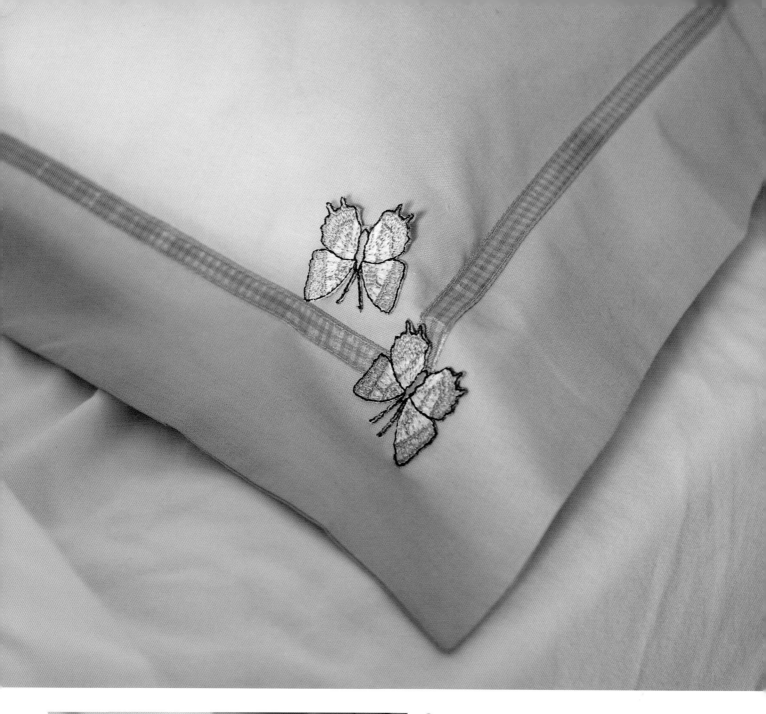

3 Use an air-erasable pen and a ruler to draw a border 5 cm (2 in) wide inside the outer edges to form a flange. Follow the **Applying Ribbon and Turning Ribbon Corners techniques** on pages 96–97 to stitch the gingham ribbon to the pillowcase, matching the outer edge of the ribbon to the drawn lines. Press or hand sew the embroidered butterfly motifs to one corner of the ribbon.

YOU WILL NEED

- 112 cm (44 in) wide lilac patterned cotton fabric (quantity depends on size of tablecloth)
- 112 cm (44 in) wide lilac spotted cotton fabric (quantity depends on size of tablecloth)
- White pompon edging (quantity depends on size of tablecloth)

CUTTING OUT

From lilac patterned cotton fabric, cut:

- See Step 1 below, then fold the fabric into quarters. Pin the circle pattern on top, matching the straight edges to the folds. Cut out the circle.

From lilac spotted cotton fabric, cut:

- See Step 1 to cut four quarter circles. These will be sewn together to make the border.

Round tablecloth

Choose two pretty patterned fabrics to make this circular tablecloth with its deep border, which has a funky pompon trimming inserted into the seam. You can tailor-make the tablecloth to suit whatever size table you have by following the straightforward instructions below.

1 Measure the diameter of the table, then measure the drop required for the cloth. The diameter of the tablecloth will be the diameter of the table plus twice the drop measurement. Follow the **Making a Circular Pattern technique** on page 24 to make a quarter circle pattern, but don't cut it out yet.

Decide on the depth of your border, adjust the length of string and draw the border within the quarter circle pattern. Trace the border line onto tracing paper or greaseproof (wax) paper. Add a 1.5 cm (⅝ in) seam allowance to the edges and draw the grain line parallel with the straight edges of the quarter circle. Cut out the border pattern.

On the original drawing, add a 1.5 cm (⅝ in) seam allowance to the border line on the circle. Cut out to use as a pattern (see **Cutting Out** left).

2 Pin white pompon edging to the circumference of the fabric circle on the right side, placing the top of the pompons at least 1.5 cm (⅝ in) from the raw edge to accommodate the seam allowance when the seam is stitched. Tack (baste) in place, use a zipper foot or piping foot if machine stitching. Overlap the ends of the pompon trim by 2 cm (¾ in). Divide the circumference of the circle into quarters and mark with a pin.

3 Follow the **Sewing a Flat Felled Seam technique** on page 29 to join the borders, forming a ring. With right sides facing, pin the circle to the border, matching the pins to the seams. Stitch in place with a zipper foot or piping foot on the sewing machine, taking a 1.5 cm (⅝ in) seam allowance. Neaten the seam with a zigzag stitch, following the **Neatening Seams technique** on page 36, and press the seam towards the circle.

4 Tack the circumference of the border by machine 5 mm (¼ in) from the raw edge, starting and finishing at each seam. Pin up a 1.5 cm (⅝ in) hem on the border and tack (baste) by machine close to the folded edge. Gently draw up the first row of tacking (basting) to ease the hem so that the eased fabric lays flat.

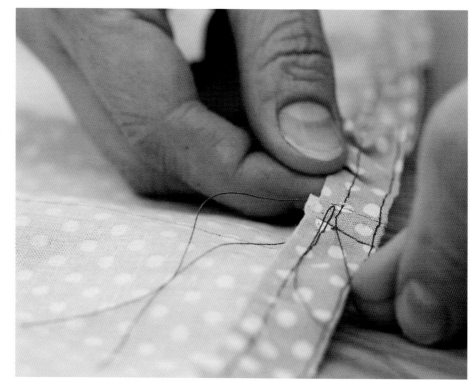

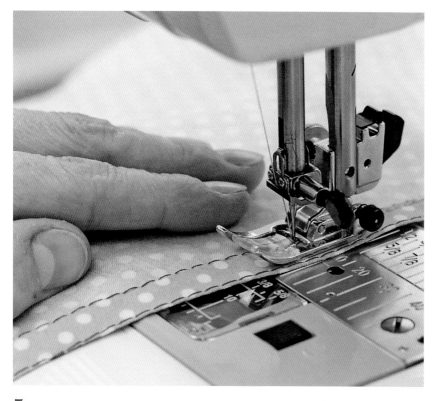

5 Press the hem, then turn under the raw edge along the eased tacking. Machine stitch close to the inner edge of the hem. Remove both rows of tacking (basting).

Round tablecloth detail

Zigzag stitching

Use an open zigzag stitch to neaten the raw edges of seams or to zigzag over a length of yarn to couch it to a fabric—see the Wavy Line throw on pages 98–99. Zigzag stitching is also great for decorative purposes. Closely worked zigzag stitching applied to raw fabric edges will conceal the edges and can be used to outline shapes cut from fabric or to appliqué a fabric shape onto a background fabric to minimize fraying.

Neatening Seams

Protect raw edges of seams that will be prone to wear with a zigzag stitch. The seams can be neatened before or after they are stitched. If you think you may alter the size of an item, zigzag the seam after it has been stitched.

Always test zigzag stitching on a scrap of fabric first. Set the stitch width to about 3 mm (⅛ in) wide and 3 mm (⅛ in) long, then stitch along the raw edges.

Zigzag Edging

A layer of tear-away stabilizer under the zigzag stitching will add stability and is recommended when working a close zigzag stitch.

1. On the right side of the fabric, draw the outline to be stitched with air-erasable pen or a fine, sharp pencil, allowing a margin of about 3 cm (1¼ in) outside the outline. Pin pieces of tear-away stabilizer under the outline—the stabilizer should extend at least 1.2 cm (½ in) either side of the outline. Stitch along the outline with a straight stitch.

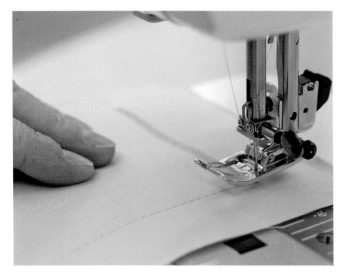

② Set the stitch width to a 4 mm (³⁄₁₆ in) wide close zigzag stitch. Stitch along the outline with the straight stitching centred. To turn the stitching at a corner, stitch to 2 mm (¹⁄₁₂ in) beyond the straight stitching. Take your foot of the power and keep the needle inserted at the outside edge of the corner, lift the presser foot and pivot the fabric. Lower the presser foot and continue stitching the next edge. To finish a continuous outline, overlap the start of the zigzagging by about 1 cm (³⁄₈ in).

③ Don't cut off the trailing threads at the start and finish of the zigzagging. Instead, pull the threads to the wrong side, then insert the thread ends into a needle and work the threads through the back of the zigzag stitching for about 3 cm (1¼ in). Now cut off the excess threads.

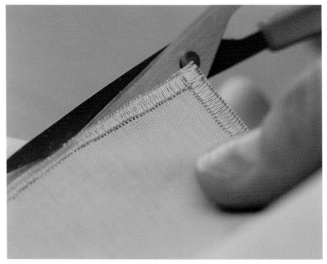

④ Gently pull away the tear-away stabilizer on each side of the zigzag stitching.

⑤ Carefully trim away the excess fabric outside the zigzag stitching with a pair of sharp embroidery scissors.

Zigzag flower mat

This pop art-inspired place mat has a chic yet light-hearted quality. The scalloped edges are neatened with a close zigzag stitch using machine embroidery thread. See the **Making a Scallop Edging technique** on page 92 to add a scalloped edge to a straight-sided shape, or have fun making mats in other bold shapes, such as leaves or clouds.

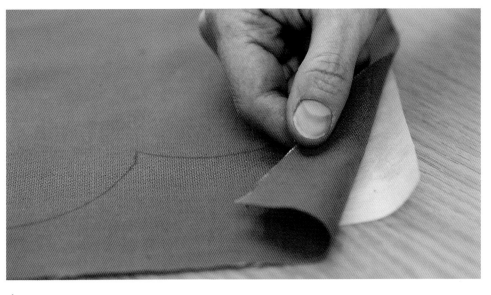

1 Use the template on page 138 to draw the place mat on the right side of the pink fabric rectangle using an air-erasable pen or a fine, sharp pencil. Pin the stabilizer underneath.

Tip: Shaded, metallic and holographic machine embroidery thread is now available. Specialist suppliers even stock glow-in-the-dark machine embroidery thread, which would certainly add an atmospheric touch to a set of place mats at a late night supper party!

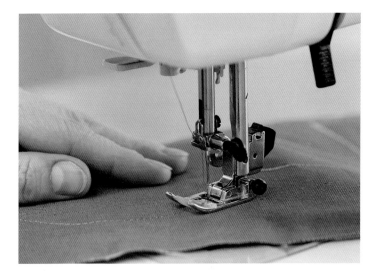

2 Follow the **Zigzag Edging technique** on pages 36–37 to make the place mat, gently guiding the fabric under the needle as you stitch the curves.

Gussets

A gusset is a band of fabric stitched between a front and back or a top and base piece of fabric in order to create a three-dimensional item, such as a rectangular or round box or a bag. You can use this technique to create the soft cuffed box and shopping bag on the following pages.

Turning Gusset Corners

1 With right sides facing, stitch the gussets together, starting and finishing the seam at the upper and lower seam allowances. Press the seams open.

2 Pin the gussets to the main piece of fabric, matching the corners. Stitch, pivoting the seam at the corners.

3 Clip the corners and then press the seam open.

Applying a Gusset to a Circle

1 With right sides facing, stitch the ends of the gussets together, forming a ring. Press the seam open.

2 Fold the circle and one edge of the gusset into quarters, then mark the edges of the fabric with a pin at each quarter mark. If the circle is small, snip the seam allowance of the gusset at regular intervals—this will help the seam allowance to lay flat when stitched to the curve. With right sides facing, pin the circle to one edge of the gusset, matching the quarter marks.

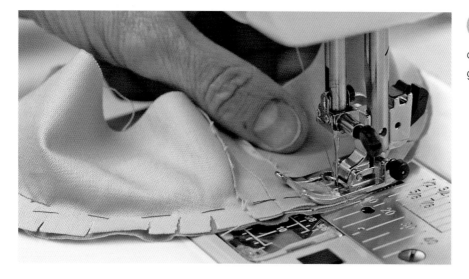

3 Tack (baste) the seam, then stitch in place. Snip the curves. Press the seam towards the gusset.

Soft cuffed box

Soft cuffed box

YOU WILL NEED

- 50 cm (⅔ yd) of 90 cm (36 in) wide iron-on medium loft fleece
- 50 cm (⅔ yd) of 137 cm (54 in) wide aqua spotted soft furnishing fabric
- 50 cm (⅔ yd) of 137 cm (54 in) wide blue striped soft furnishing fabric
- 29.5 x 20.5 cm (11¾ x 8 in) rectangle of thin plastic or mounting board

CUTTING OUT

From iron-on medium loft fleece, cut:

- Two 23 x 22 cm (9 x 8⅝ in) rectangles for the box sides
- Two 31 x 22 cm (12⅜ x 8⅝ in) rectangles for the box front and back
- One 31 x 22 cm (12⅜ x 8⅝ in) rectangle for the base

From aqua spotted and blue striped soft furnishing fabric, cut:

- Two 24 x 23 cm (9⅜ x 9 in) rectangles for the box sides
- Two 32 x 23 cm (12¾ x 9 in) rectangles for the box front and back
- One 32 x 23 cm (12¾ x 9 in) rectangle for the base

This tactile storage box is a contemporary take on the humble workbox. The fabric box is ideal for storing sewing and knitting projects because it is softly padded for added protection. The padding is created with iron-on medium loft fleece (see page 16), which is cut smaller than the fabric pieces to reduce the bulk in the seam allowances.

1 Press iron-on medium loft fleece centrally to the wrong side of the aqua spotted pieces. With right sides facing and taking a 1 cm (⅜ in) seam allowance, stitch each aqua spotted box side between the aqua spotted box front and back along the short edges, finishing the seam 1 cm (⅜ in) above the lower edges, forming a ring. Repeat to join the blue striped box sides between the front and back. Press the seams open.

Tip: When stitching the aqua spotted and blue striped box pieces together, you may find it easier to remove the bed of the sewing machine.

2 With right sides facing and taking a 1 cm (⅜ in) seam allowance, pin and stitch the aqua spotted and blue striped box sides, front and back together along the long upper edges, matching the seams. Turn right side out, with the aqua spotted side outside. Press the upper edge. Tack (baste) the lower, raw edges together.

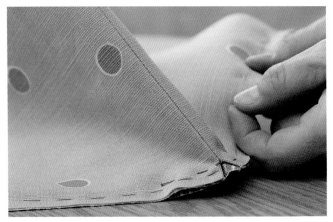

3 With the right sides of the blue striped fabric pieces facing, pin the striped base to the lower edge of the box, matching the seams to the corners of the base. Taking a 1 cm (⅜ in) seam allowance, follow Steps 2–3 of the **Turning Gusset Corners technique** on page 40 to stitch the box to the base. Press the seam towards the base. Press under 1 cm (⅜ in) on all the edges of the aqua spotted base. With wrong sides facing, place the aqua spotted base on the base of the box, matching the corners. Pin the adjacent pressed edges to the seam.

4 Slipstitch the pressed edges to the seam along one long and one short edge (see page 25). Slip the plastic or board rectangle used for stiffening between the bases and adjust the seam allowance to lie on top of the card. Pin and slipstitch remaining pressed edges along the base seam, enclosing the stiffening. Turn the blue striped side of the box to the outside for 5 cm (2 in) to form the cuff.

YOU WILL NEED

- 50 cm (⅔ yd) of 112 cm (44 in) wide green striped cotton fabric
- 20 cm (¼ yd) of 90 cm (36 in) wide iron-on firm interfacing
- 50 cm (⅔ yd) of 112 cm (44 in) wide turquoise patterned cotton fabric
- 50 cm (⅔ yd) of 112 cm (44 in) wide green patterned cotton fabric
- 50 cm (⅔ yd) of 90 cm (36 in) wide iron-on firm flexible interfacing

CUTTING OUT

From green striped cotton fabric, cut:

- Two 55 x 10 cm (21½ x 4 in) strips for handles
- Two 40 x 36 cm (15¾ x 14¼ in) rectangles for the front and back lining
- Two 40 x 8 cm (15¾ x 3¼ in) for side gusset linings
- One 36 x 8 cm (14¼ x 3¼ in) rectangle for the base gusset lining

From iron-on firm interfacing, cut:

- Two 55 x 10 cm (21½ x 4 in) strips for handles

From turquoise patterned cotton fabric and iron-on firm flexible interfacing, cut:

- Two 40 x 36 cm (15¾ x 14¼ in) rectangles for the front and back

From green patterned cotton fabric and iron-on firm flexible interfacing, cut:

- Two 40 x 8 cm (15¾ x 3¼ in) rectangles for side gussets
- One 36 x 8 cm (14¼ x 3¼ in) rectangle for the base gusset

Shopping bag

Dealing with the shopping is much more fun when you have a smart bag to carry the load. The bag is made from three different yet coordinating fabrics, so it's an ideal project for using up colourful remnants. It measures 38 cm (15 in) high, excluding the handles, and 34 cm (13½ in) wide.

 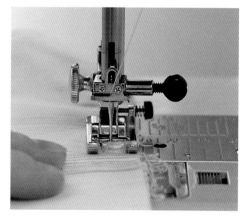

1 Press the interfacing to the wrong side of the fabric pieces. Follow the **Making a Handle and Stitching Ends techniques** on page 76 to make the handles and then pin and stitch the ends to the right side of the front and back, positioning them 9.5 cm (3¾ in) below the short upper edges and 8 cm (3¼ in) in from the long side edges.

2 Follow the **Turning Gusset Corners technique** on page 40 to stitch the side and base gussets to the long side edges and short lower edges of the front and back. Press the seams open. Make the lining in the same way, but leave a 20 cm (8 in) gap in one side gusset seam to turn right side out. Turn the bag right side out and slip it into the lining with right sides facing, matching the seams. Pin and stitch the upper raw edges taking a 1 cm (⅜ in) seam allowance.

3 Turn the lining to the right side, then slipstitch the gap closed (see page 25). Push the lining into the bag and press the upper edge. Topstitch 7.5 mm (5⁄16 in) below the upper edge.

Hems

There are many occasions when you will need to hem fabric, either by hand or machine, to stop the raw edge fraying and to ensure a neat appearance, and it pays off to do the job properly.

Making a Plain Hem

① First press under 1 cm (⅜ in) of the raw fabric edge, and then press under the depth of the hem.

② If you need to turn a corner, open out the fabric at the corner and cut diagonally across the allowance 6 mm (¼ in) from the corner.

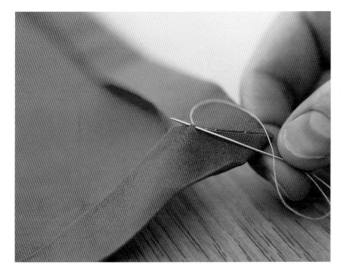

③ Turn the diagonal edge under, then refold the hem—the diagonal folded edges should meet edge to edge. Slipstitch the mitred edges together (see page 25).

④ Stitch close to the inner pressed edges of the entire hem with your sewing machine. Alternatively, slipstitch the hem in place by hand.

Making a Curtain Hem

1 After hemming the side edges of the curtain, fold up a 2 cm (¾ in) and then an 8 cm (3¼ in) hem on the lower edge. Mark the outer corner with a pin. With another pin, mark the point where the lower hem meets the side hem at the inner edges.

2 Unfold the hem once at the corner. Fold the corner at an angle between the pins, then refold the hem. Slipstitch the mitred corner edge in place (see page 25). Slipstitch the hem of an unlined curtain, but use herringbone stitch for the hem of a lined or interlined curtain (see page 25).

YOU WILL NEED

- Cream hand towel
- Approximately 40 cm (½ yd) of 112 cm (44 in) wide turquoise patterned cotton fabric
- Approximately 1.2 m (1½ yd) of beige 1.5 cm (⅝ in) wide ric-rac

CUTTING OUT

Measure the width of the towel. Decide on the depth you would like the fabric borders to be—those on this towel are 10 cm (4 in) deep. Many towels have a woven band just above the short edges; if so, measure the depth from the top of the woven band to the lower edge of the towel.

From turquoise patterned cotton fabric, cut:

- Two rectangles that are the towel width plus 6 cm (2½ in) x the border depth measurement plus 4 cm (1½ in) for the turnings/ hems

Towel with borders

Customize a plain towel by adding colourful fabric borders finished off with ric-rac trimming. A neatly mitred hem on the underside makes sure that the towel looks good on both sides. A set of these towels with borders would make a lovely housewarming present.

1 Press under 1 cm (⅜ in) on the long upper edges of the borders. On the right side, tack (baste) a length of 1.5 cm (⅝ in) wide ric-rac along the pressed edge.

2 Follow Steps 1–3 of the **Making a Plain Hem technique** on page 46 to press a hem on the raw edges of the borders and mitre the corners— the depth of the hem should be 2 cm (¾ in). Slip the short edges and corners of the towel into the pressed hem edges and corners, then pin the hemmed edges to the towel.

3 Turn the towel over and smooth out the fabric, then pin the upper edge of the borders to the towel. Slipstitch the hems to the towel (see page 25).

4 Stitch along the centre of the ric-rac with your sewing machine, stitching through both the border and towel.

YOU WILL NEED

- 1.3 m (1½ yd) of 90 cm (36 in) wide iron-on firm flexible interfacing
- 90 cm (1 yd) of 150 cm (60 in) wide pale pink wool fabric or felted wool
- 50 cm (⅔ yd) of 150 cm (60 in) wide mid pink wool fabric or felted wool
- Strong cream thread

CUTTING OUT

From iron-on firm flexible interfacing, cut:

- One 120 x 75 cm (47½ x 30 in) rectangle for the backing

From pale pink wool fabric or felted wool, cut:

- One 85 x 24 cm (34 x 9½ in) rectangle for the centre band
- Two 85 x 29 cm (34 x 11½ in) rectangles for the end bands

From mid pink wool fabric or felted wool, cut:

- Two 85 x 24 cm (34 x 9½ in) rectangles for the middle bands

Striped rug

Add a cosy yet stylish touch to your décor with this wool rug. The smart stripes are achieved by fusing bands of woollen fabrics in toning colours to a backing of interfacing, then oversewing the joins with a large herringbone stitch. The rug measures 120 × 75 cm (48 × 30 in). Cut the bands carefully along the grain of the fabric to keep the edges neat.

1 Lay the centre band on the ironing board, wrong side up. Using a fine, sharp pencil or an air-erasable pen, lightly draw lines across the backing on the right side 24 cm (9½ in) apart, parallel with the short edges. Position the backing on top, adhesive side down, matching the drawn centre lines to the long edges of the band, allowing each of the short edges of the band to extend 5 cm (2 in) beyond the long edges of the backing. Press the interfacing to the band to fuse the layers together. Take care not to fuse the interfacing material to the ironing board.

2 Lift the ends of the backing and position a middle band each side of the centre band, butting the long edges together and the short edges level. Replace the backing and fuse in place as before. Lift each end of the backing and position an end band either side of the middle bands, butting the long edges together with the outer edges extending 5 cm (2 in) beyond the edges of the backing. Replace the backing and fuse in place as before. Check that the fabric is fully fused to the backing.

3 Starting and finishing 5 cm (2 in) from the raw edges of the bands, use strong cream thread to work herringbone stitch over the joins of the bands (see page 25). Oversew the extending raw edges of the joins with sewing thread.

> **Tip:** To keep the herringbone stitches even, use an air-erasable pen to draw lines 1 cm (³⁄₈ in) from and parallel with the joins, then work the herringbone stitches between the drawn lines.

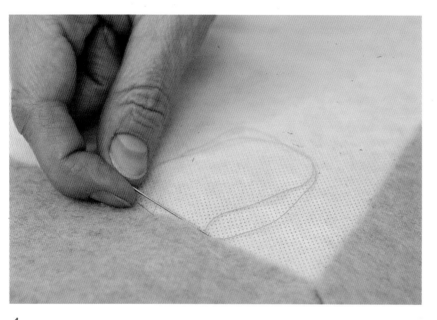

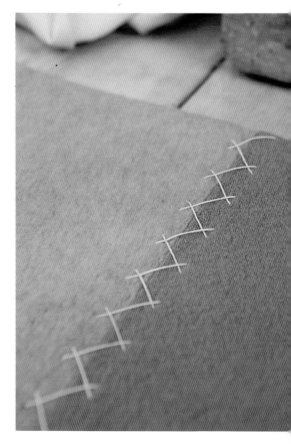

4 Press the raw edges to the wrong side for 5 cm (2 in). Follow Steps 2–3 of the **Making a Plain Hem technique** on page 48 to hem the rug. Secure the hem in place with herringbone stitch using sewing thread, taking care not to sew through to the right side of the rug.

Right: *Striped rug stitching detail*

YOU WILL NEED

- 137 cm (54 in) wide pink and pale green on cream striped soft furnishing fabric (quantity depends on size of stool)
- 2.5 cm (1 in) wide pink grosgrain ribbon (quantity depends on size of stool)

CUTTING OUT

Measure the length and width of the top of the stool. Measure the drop of the cover required, that is how far down the legs you would like the cover to hang, which should be 2.5 cm (1 in) below the base of the seat.

From pink and pale green on cream striped soft furnishing fabric, cut:

- One rectangle or square that is the length plus twice the drop plus 6 cm (2½ in) x the width plus twice the drop plus 6 cm (2½ in) for the cover

Slip-over stool cover

A slip-over cover for an old rectangular or square stool will completely transform its appearance from care-worn to cutting edge. It's easy to achieve a custom fit and only a small amount of stitching is required. A band of ribbon stitched along the lower edge, picking up on one of the colours of the fabric, adds the perfect finishing touch. The cover can be removed for laundering.

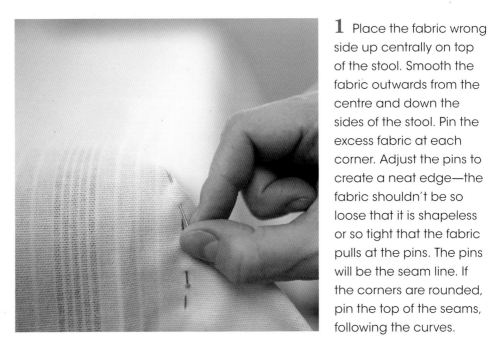

1 Place the fabric wrong side up centrally on top of the stool. Smooth the fabric outwards from the centre and down the sides of the stool. Pin the excess fabric at each corner. Adjust the pins to create a neat edge—the fabric shouldn't be so loose that it is shapeless or so tight that the fabric pulls at the pins. The pins will be the seam line. If the corners are rounded, pin the top of the seams, following the curves.

2 When you are happy with the fit, make sure that there are no loose pins and remove the cover. Cut away the excess fabric beyond the pins, leaving a 1.5 cm (⅝ in) seam allowance.

3 Stitch the seams as pinned. Neaten the seam allowance with a zigzag stitch, following the **Neatening Seams technique** on page 36. Press the seams open. Slip the cover over the stool and pin up the hem, then remove the cover. Cut the lower edge, leaving a 2.7 cm (1⅛ in) allowance below the desired drop of the cover. Follow the **Making a Plain Hem technique** on page 46 to make a 2 cm (¾ in) deep hem.

4 On the right side, pin the grosgrain ribbon to the lower edge of the cover with the lower edge of the ribbon extending 3 mm (⅛ in) below the hem. Cut off the excess ribbon 3 cm (1¼ in) beyond the start of the ribbon. Turn the end under for 1 cm (⅜ in) and pin to the cover, overlapping the start of the ribbon. Stitch close to the upper edge of the ribbon. Slipstitch the overlapped ends of the ribbon together (see page 25).

Bias bindings

Bindings are used to neaten raw edges, and can either be discreet by choosing fabric to match the fabric it is neatening or made into a feature with a contrast fabric. Straight bindings (cut parallel with the warp or weft of the fabric) can be used to bind the straight edges of fabric, while bias binding (cut on the bias of the fabric) is suitable for either curved or straight edges.

Cutting Bias Strips

The bias is any direction on the fabric that is not the warp or weft. Strips of fabric cut on the bias can be used to make bias binding, rouleaux (see page 77) and piping (see page 60). The bias will cause the seams to stretch, so take care when stitching.

Fold the fabric diagonally at a 45-degree angle to the selvedge. Press along the fold, then open out flat. For bindings and piping, add 10 cm (4 in) to the desired length for easing the strip around curves and corners as well as for neatening the ends. Add a 6 mm (¼ in) seam allowance for joins. Use an air-erasable pen, water-soluble pen or sharp tailor's chalk and a ruler to draw lines the width of the bias strip parallel with the pressed line, then cut out the strips.

Joining Bias Strips

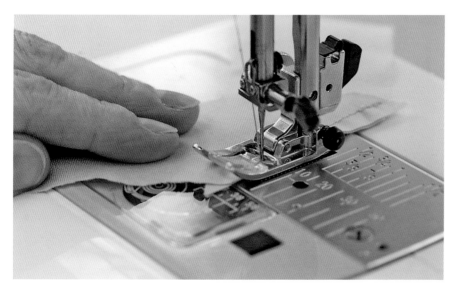

With right sides facing, position one end of two bias strips at right angles, matching the ends. Stitch the strips together, taking a 6 mm (¼ in) seam allowance. Press the seam open and snip off the extending corners.

Making Bias Binding

Although ready-made bias binding is available, it is quick, easy and economical to make your own using a bias binding maker (see page 12). This simple metal gadget comes in different sizes to make 1.2 cm (½ in), 1.8 cm (¾ in), 2.5 cm (1 in) and 5 cm (2 in) wide binding. The manufacturer's instructions will indicate the width to cut the binding.

Resting on an ironing board, push a bias or straight strip of fabric through the wide end of a bias binding maker. The edges will be turned under as the binding emerges out of the narrow end; press in place as you pull the binding through.

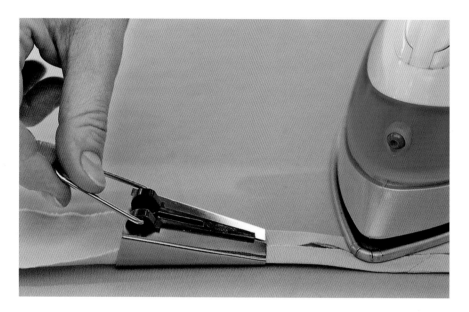

Binding a Circumference

Open out one folded edge of the binding. Turn under the end of the binding to start. With right sides facing, pin the binding to the fabric, matching the raw edges. Pin along the fold line, then cut off the excess binding 1 cm (⅜ in) beyond the start of the binding. Overlap the ends of the strips. Stitch along the fold line.

Binding a Straight Edge

Pin the binding to the fabric, matching the raw edges with right sides facing and with the end of the binding extending at least 1 cm (⅜ in) beyond the start of the edge to be bound. Stitch along the fold line. Cut off the excess binding 1 cm (⅜ in) beyond the ends of the seam. Turn under both ends of the binding and secure with a pin.

Finishing Binding

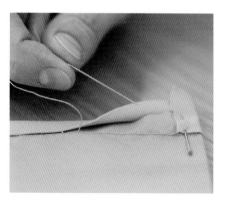

Turn the binding to the underside, enclosing the raw edges and matching the pressed edge to the seam. Pin along the seam. Alternatively, turn up the bias binding so that it is not visible on the right side and pin in place. Slipstitch or stitch along the pressed edge. Slipstitch the ends of the binding in place (see page 25).

YOU WILL NEED

- 40 cm (½ yd) of 112 cm (44 in) wide blue patterned cotton fabric
- 30 cm (⅓ yd) of 90 cm (36 in) wide 2 oz wadding (batting)
- 60 cm (⅔ yd) of 112 cm (44 in) wide lilac cotton fabric
- 1.8 cm (¾ in) bias binding maker
- 1.5 cm (⅝ in) shell button

CUTTING OUT

Refer to the pattern on page 140 to cut from blue patterned cotton fabric and 2 oz wadding (batting):

- Two cafetière cosies

From lilac cotton fabric, cut:

- Two cafetière cosies
- One 76 x 3.5 cm (30 x 1⅜ in) length of bias binding (see the **Cutting Bias Strips technique** on page 56)
- One 18 x 3 cm (7 x 1¼ in) bias strip for the loop

Cafetière cosy

Keep a cafetière of coffee nicely hot while looking cool with this smart cosy, which is purpose-designed with padding for efficient insulation. The edges are finished with toning handcrafted bias binding, and the cosy also features a handy loop trimmed with a decorative button for hanging.

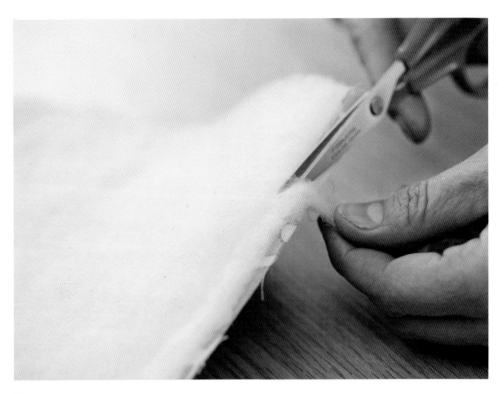

1 Pin each blue patterned cafetière cosy right side up on the wadding (batting) cosy. With right sides facing, pin the lilac cosies on top. Stitch together along the lower straight edge, taking a 1 cm (⅜ in) seam allowance. Carefully trim away the wadding (batting) in the seam allowance. Turn the lilac cover to the underside. Pin the raw edges together, enclosing the wadding (batting). Press the stitched edges.

> **Tip:** If your patterned fabric has a distinctive motif, see the **Positioning Motifs technique** on page 22 to centre the motif—but you may need to allow extra fabric for this.

2 Place the covers together with the patterned covers facing outwards. Pin and tack the outer raw edges together. Refer to the **Making Bias Binding**, **Binding a Straight Edge** and **Finishing Binding techniques** on pages 56–57 to bind the raw edges of the cover with the lilac bias binding.

3 Follow the **Making a Rouleau technique** on page 77 to make the loop, slipstitching the ends closed. Overlap the ends of the loop by 2.5 cm (1 in) and sew to the top of the cover. Sew the button on top.

Piping

Use piping to define a seam. Ready-made piping is available only in a limited range of colours and is costly, but making your own piping is easy using inexpensive piping cord and covering it with a strip of fabric. There is an endless choice of fabrics and colours to choose from, to match or contrast with the main fabric.

Making Piping

1 Measure the circumference of the piping cord with a tape measure and add 3 cm (1¼ in) for seam allowances. Cut a bias strip of fabric in this width that is the length required plus 10 cm (4 in) for ease and joining, following the Cutting Bias Strips technique on page 56. Join bias strips if necessary—see the **Joining Bias Strips technique** on page 56.

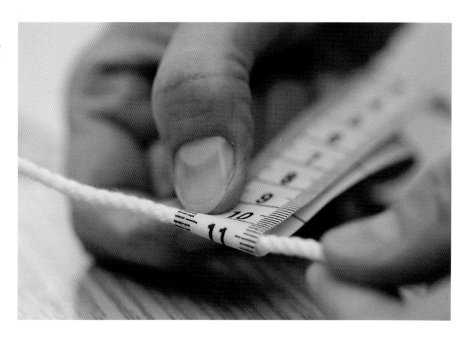

2 Lay the cord along the centre of the bias strip on the wrong side. Set the sewing machine to a long straight stitch length for machine tacking (basting). Fold the strip lengthways in half, enclosing the cord. Using a piping foot or zipper foot, stitch close to the piping cord with matching sewing thread.

Pinning Curves and Joining Piping Ends

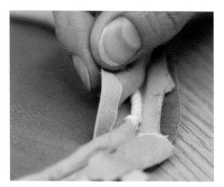

1 To join the ends of piping, if piping a circle for instance, allow a 2.5 cm (1 in) overlap. With the raw edges level, pin the piping to the right side of the fabric to 5 cm (2 in) each side of the overlap. If pinning to a curved edge, snip the seam allowance so that it lays flat. Unpick the piping tacking (basting) for 5 cm (2 in) either side of the overlap to reveal the cord. Unravel the cord ends and cut 2.5 cm (1 in) from half the strands at each end of the cord to thin it.

2 Twist the ends of the cord together and bind with thread. Secure in place with a few stitches to hold the cord together.

3 Wrap one end of the piping strip around the cord again. Turn under 6 mm (¼ in) on the other end and wrap it around the cord. Pin and tack (baste) in place ready for stitching.

Turning Piping Corners

Start to pin the piping to the right side of the fabric, matching the raw edges. When you reach the corner, snip the seam allowance of the piping to fit the corner. Continue pinning the piping, then tack (baste) in place ready for stitching.

YOU WILL NEED

- 137 cm (54 in) wide curtain lining (quantity depends on size of headboard)
- 2 cm (¾ in) wide sew-on hook and loop closure tape (quantity depends on size of headboard)
- 60 cm (⅔ yd) of 137 cm (54 in) wide blue striped soft furnishing fabric
- 3 mm (⅛ in) diameter piping cord (quantity depends on size of headboard)
- 137 cm (54 in) wide blue check soft furnishing fabric (quantity depends on size of headboard)
- 2.4 m (2¾ yd) of 1.5 cm (⅝ in) wide cotton tape

CUTTING OUT

Measure the width (A), height (B) and thickness (C) of the headboard.

From curtain lining, cut:

- Two half A plus 6 cm (2⅜ in) x B plus 4 cm (1½ in) rectangles for the right- and left-hand backs

From blue striped soft furnishing fabric:

- Two 4 cm (1½ in) wide bias strips measuring A plus twice B plus 4 cm (1½ in) for the piping (see the **Cutting Bias Strips** and **Joining Bias Strips** techniques on page 56)

From blue check soft furnishing fabric, cut:

- One A plus 3 cm (1¼ in) x B plus 4 cm (1½ in) rectangle for the front
- One A plus 3 cm (1¼ in) x C plus 3 cm (1¼ in) strip for the top gusset
- Two B plus 4 cm (1½ in) x C plus 3 cm (1¼ in) strips for the side gussets

Headboard cover

Give a new lease of life to a tired or dull headboard with this clean-cut and fresh-looking slip-over cover. These instructions are for a rectangular or square flat-fronted headboard. Contrast piping gives a really professional finish to the cover, which can be easily removed for laundering. Unscrew the battens from the back of the headboard before you begin.

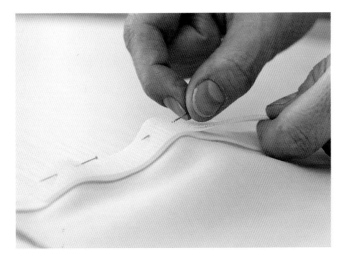

1 For the right-hand back, press under 1 cm (⅜ in) and then 2 cm (¾ in) on one B measurement edge of one back rectangle, then tack (baste) across the upper and lower edges. Cut a length of hook and loop closure tape 6 cm (2⅜ in) shorter than measurement B. Starting 2 cm (¾ in) below the top edge, pin one section of the tape to the pressed edge on the wrong side.

2 For the left-hand back, press under 1 cm (⅜ in) and then 2.5 cm (1 in) on one B measurement edge of the other back rectangle. Starting 2 cm (¾ in) below the top edge, pin the other section of the hook and loop closure tape close to the pressed edge on the right side. Tack (baste) across the upper and lower edges. Stitch close to the long edges and across the ends of both tape sections. With right sides facing up, lap the right-hand back over the left-hand back to fasten the tape. Tack the overlapped edges together at the upper edge.

3 Follow the **Making Piping technique** on page 60 to make two lengths of piping using the bias strips. Pin and tack (baste) the piping to the side and top edges of the front and back, following the **Turning Piping Corners technique** on page 61, bending each end of the piping to keep it 4 cm (1½ in) above the lower edges of the front and back.

4 Following the **Turning Gusset Corners technique** on page 40, stitch the top gusset between the side gussets and then use a zipper foot or piping foot on the sewing machine to stitch the gusset between the front and back. Layer the seam, referring to the **Layering Seams technique** on page 29. Press the seams towards the gusset. Press under 1 cm (⅜ in) and then 1.5 cm (⅝ in) on the lower edges. Stitch close to the inner pressed edges to hem the headboard cover.

5 For the ties, cut eight 30 cm (12 in) lengths of the cotton tape. Follow the **Stitching Ends technique** on page 76 to stitch each tie 3.5 cm (1⅜ in) above the hemmed edge, positioning the ties 11 cm (4½ in) in from the side and opening edges on the wrong side of the back. Stitch ties in corresponding positions on the wrong side of the front. Slip the headboard cover over the headboard, press the hook and loop closure tape sections together and fasten the ties together in a bow under the headboard. Screw the battens to the back of the headboard and screw to the end of the bed.

YOU WILL NEED

- 60 cm (⅔ yd) of 112 cm (44 in) wide blue on fawn patterned cotton fabric
- 60 cm (⅔ yd) of 112 cm (44 in) wide green spotted cotton fabric
- 30 cm (⅓ yd) of 112 cm (44 in) wide multicoloured striped cotton fabric
- 30 cm (⅓ yd) of 112 cm (44 in) wide blue striped cotton fabric
- 40 cm (16 in) zip (zipper)
- 1.2 m (1⅓ yd) of 3 mm (⅛ in) diameter piping cord
- 45 x 17 cm (18 x 6¾ in) bolster cushion pad

CUTTING OUT

From blue on fawn patterned cotton fabric, cut:

- One 55 x 22 cm (21⅝ x 8⅝ in) rectangle for the centre panel

From green spotted cotton fabric, cut:

- Two 55 x 16 cm (21⅝ x 6¼ in) rectangles for the side panels

From multicoloured striped cotton fabric, cut:

- Two 59 x 4 cm (23¼ x 1½ in) bias strips for the piping

From blue striped cotton fabric, cut:

- Two 20 cm (8 in) diameter circles for the end circles

Bolster cushion

This fabulous bolster cushion features four coordinating patterned fabrics, which makes it another great project for putting your fabric remnants to creative use. Neat rings of piping encircle either end of the cushion to emphasize its rounded shape. The cover simply unzips for laundering.

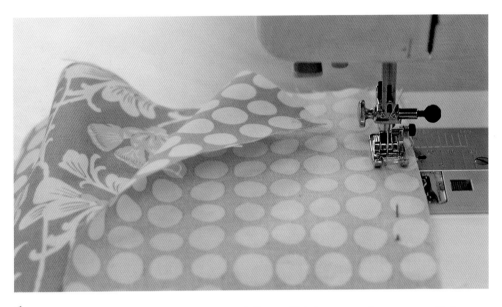

1 With right sides facing and taking a 1.5 cm (⅝ in) seam allowance, stitch the centre panel between the side panels along the long edges. Press the seams open. With right sides facing, fold the panelled cushion in half parallel with the short edges, matching the seams. Refer to the **Inserting a Zip (Zipper) technique** on pages 72–73 to sew the zip (zipper) into the short edges. Open the zip (zipper).

2 Follow the **Making Piping technique** on page 60 to make two 59 cm (23¼ in) lengths of piping using the bias strips. Apply the piping to the circumference of the end circles, following the **Pinning Curves and Joining Piping Ends technique** on page 61. Follow Step 2 of the **Applying a Gusset to a Circle technique** on page 41 to pin the ends of the tube to the circles.

3 Taking a 1.5 cm (⅝ in) seam allowance, follow Step 3 of the **Applying a Gusset to a Circle technique** to tack (baste) and stitch the circles to the tube using a zipper foot or piping foot on your sewing machine. Layer the seam, following the **Layering Seams technique** on page 29. Turn right side out. Insert the cushion pad and close the zip (zipper).

Tip: When inserting the zip (zipper), take care that you don't stitch through to the underside of the tube.

Envelope opening

An envelope opening is a flap that closes over the front or back of cushions or duvet (comforter) covers. You can instantly make a feature of an envelope opening by using a contrast fabric or adding buttonholes or loops for fastening.

Making an Envelope Opening

The finished depth of the flap must be at least 10.5 cm (4⅛ in) to cover the hemmed edge of the front. Cut two rectangles of fabric that measure the depth of the flap x one finished side edge of a cushion or the finished width of a duvet (comforter) cover with a 1.5 cm (⅝ in) seam allowance added to all edges.

Tip: The front and back are cut the same size, but if you want a particularly deep flap, cut the front shorter so that it will be easy to slip the cushion pad or duvet (comforter) into.

1 If the flap is to fasten with loops, tack (baste) them to the right side of one flap now. With right sides facing and taking a 1.5 cm (⅝ in) seam allowance, stitch the flaps together along one long edge (the tacked or basted edge if using loops).

2 Turn the flap right side out and pin the raw edges together. If needed, make buttonholes along the stitched edge of the flap now.

3 With right sides facing, pin the flap to one edge of the back, matching the raw edges.

4 On the front, press under 1 cm (⅜ in) and then 4 cm (1½ in) on the edge that will have the flap opening. Stitch close to the inner pressed edge to hem the front.

5 With right sides facing, pin the front to the back, matching the raw edges and overlapping the hemmed edge of the front over the flap.

6 Stitch the outer edges, taking a 1.5 cm (⅝ in) seam allowance. Clip the corners and turn right side out, turning the flap over the front.

Envelope duvet cover

Here, the fastening on a duvet (comforter) is elevated to a key decorative feature by using an attractive fabric to create a generous flap that closes with a set of distinctive buttons. This is also a cost-effective approach, combining a small amount of a special fabric with plain inexpensive sheeting fabric.

1 Follow the **Attaching a Button Loop technique** on page 80 to make five button loops for a single duvet (comforter) cover or seven button loops for a double cover. Working outwards from the centre of the long upper edge of the green patterned flap, mark the fabric with a pin at 20 cm (8 in) intervals to position five button loops for a single duvet (comforter) cover or seven button loops for a double cover. Tack (baste) each button loop to the right side of the flap with the pins centred.

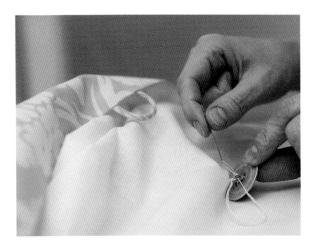

2 Follow the **Making an Envelope Opening technique** on pages 68–69, then zigzag stitch the raw edges to neaten them (see the **Neatening Seams technique** on page 36) before turning the duvet (comforter) cover right side out. Smooth the cover out flat. Mark the position of the buttons under the button loops on the front with a pin. Follow the **Sewing Buttons technique** on page 81 to sew the buttons to the cover.

YOU WILL NEED

The patterned fabric needs to be joined so that it is wide enough to make the flap, which will involve matching the design, so refer to the **Matching Patterned Fabrics technique** on page 23, remembering to allow for extra fabric.

For a single duvet (comforter) cover:
- 90 cm (1 yd) of 112 cm (44 in) wide green patterned cotton fabric
- 2.9 m (3⅓ yd) of 240 cm (94 in) wide cream cotton sheeting fabric
- Five 3 cm (1¼ in) silver buttons

For a double duvet (comforter) cover:
- 1.1 m (1⅓ yd) of 112 cm (44 in) wide green patterned cotton fabric
- 4.1 m (4½ yd) of 240 cm (94 in) wide cream cotton sheeting fabric
- Seven 3 cm (1¼ in) silver buttons

CUTTING OUT

Join the patterned fabric with a flat seam to make it large enough to cut out the flap. Press the seam open.

For a single duvet (comforter) cover, from green patterned cotton fabric, cut:
- One 143 x 42.5 cm (56¼ x 16¾ in) rectangle for the flap
- 50 x 2.5 cm (20 x 1 in) wide bias strip for button loops

For a double duvet (comforter) cover, from green patterned cotton fabric, cut:
- One 203 x 43 cm (80 x 17 in) rectangle for the flap
- 80 x 2.5 cm (31½ x 1 in) wide bias strip for button loops

For a single duvet (comforter) cover, from cream cotton sheeting fabric, cut:
- One 143 x 43 cm (56¼ x 17 in) rectangle for the flap
- One 193 x 143 cm (76 x 56¼ in) rectangle for the front
- One 203 x 143 cm (80 x 56¼ in) rectangle for the back

For a double duvet (comforter) cover, from cream cotton sheeting fabric, cut:
- One 203 x 43 cm (80 x 17 in) rectangle for the flap
- One 193 x 203 cm (76 x 80 in) rectangle for the front
- One 203 cm (80 in) square for the back

Tip: Sew metal buttons with strong thread such as button thread, as the metal may have sharp edges that could cut though ordinary sewing thread.

Zips

A zip (zipper) is a neat, inconspicuous closure for the back of a cushion, which needs to be inserted before the cushion is made up. Choose a zip that is 8 cm (3¼ in) shorter than the seam it is to be applied to. If this is not a ready-available length, use a longer zip rather than a shorter one. Allow a 1.5 cm (⅝ in) seam allowance for seams that will have a zip inserted.

Inserting a Zip (Zipper)

1 Place the zip centrally under one of the edges it is to be applied to. Mark the position of the outside edge of the top and bottom stops of the zip on the fabric with a pin.

2 With right sides facing, pin the fabric edges together. Stitch each end of the seam, finishing and starting at the pinned marks, taking a 1.5 cm (⅝ in) seam allowance.

3 Now tack (baste) the seam between the stitching, taking a 1.5 cm (⅝ in) seam allowance.

4 Press the seam open. On the wrong side, pin the zip (zipper) face down centrally along the seam, with one end of the seam level with the inside edge of the end stop at the lower end of the zip (zipper). Tack (baste) the zip (zipper) in position.

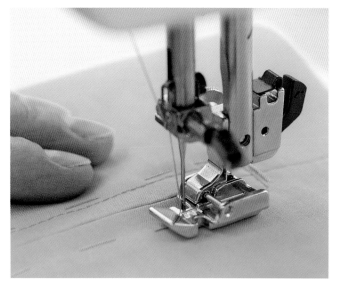

5 On the right side and starting on one side edge of the zip (zipper), use a zipper foot on your sewing machine to stitch it in place 7.5 mm (⁵⁄₁₆ in) either side of the seam and across the ends of the zip (zipper).

6 Now unpick the tacking (basting) and then open the zip (zipper). It must be open when stitching a cushion together, otherwise you won't be able to turn it right side out!

Round piped cushion

The circular shape of this striking zipped cushion is emphasized with a ring of piping on the front and back. It also features a large fabric-covered button at the centre, which dimples the fabric invitingly (you will need to snip these off for laundering, but just resew them in place afterwards). The cover will fit a standard-sized circular cushion pad.

YOU WILL NEED

- 50 cm (½ yd) of 112 cm (44 in) wide pink geometric patterned cotton fabric
- 40 cm (½ yd) of 112 cm (44 in) wide pink floral patterned cotton fabric
- 40 cm (16 in) zip (zipper)
- 2 m (2½ yd) of 3 mm (⅛ in) diameter piping cord
- 30 cm (12 in) diameter round cushion pad with 5 cm (2 in) gusset
- Two 3.8 cm (1½ in) diameter self-cover buttons
- Mattress needle
- Button thread

CUTTING OUT

From pink geometric patterned cotton fabric, cut:

- Two 50 x 5.5 cm (19¾ x 2¼ in) strips for the lower gussets
- One 50 x 8 cm (19¾ x 3¼ in) strip for the upper gusset
- 4 cm (1½ in) wide bias strips joined to make two 1 m (1¼ yd) lengths for piping

From pink floral patterned cotton fabric, cut:

- Two 33 cm (13¼ in) diameter circles for the front and back

1 Follow the **Inserting a Zip (Zipper)** technique on pages 72–73 to sew a zip (zipper) into the long edges of the lower gussets. With right sides facing, stitch the upper and lower gussets together at the short edges, forming a ring. Press the seams open. Follow the **Making Piping technique** on page 60 to make two 1 m (1¼ yd) lengths of piping using the bias strips. Apply the piping to the circumference of the front and back circles on the right side, following the **Pinning Curves and Joining Piping Ends technique** on page 61.

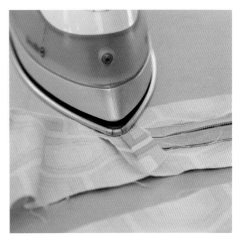

2 Taking a 1.5 cm (⅝ in) seam allowance, follow Steps 2–3 of the **Applying a Gusset to a Circle technique** on page 41 to stitch the gusset to the front circle using a zipper foot or piping foot on your sewing machine. Make sure that the zip is open, then stitch the back circle to the other edge of the gusset. Layer the seams (see the **Layering Seams technique** on page 29). Snip the curves and turn right side out. Insert the cushion pad and close the zip (zipper).

3 Follow the **Covering a Self-Cover Button technique** on page 81 to cover the two self-cover buttons with offcuts of the pink geometric patterned fabric. Mark the button positions at the centre of the front and back of the cushion with a pin. Thread the mattress needle with a 45 cm (18 in) double length of button thread. Tie the thread ends to the shank of one button. Insert the needle down through the front of the cushion at the button position and out of the button position on the back.

4 Cut off the needle. Insert one end of the thread through the shank of the other button and tie it to the other thread, pulling the threads to dimple the cushion. Tie the threads securely together. Cut off the thread ends under the button.

> **Tip:** Why not create your own cushion pad instead? Simply make the cushion from plain cotton fabric, omitting the zip, piping and buttons, and stuff with toy filling—see the **Making a Filled Shape technique** on pages 130–131.

Handles, ties and rouleaux

There are many occasions when sewing your own soft furnishing items that you will need to make handles or apply ties. In addition to their function as a fastening, ties can be added purely for decoration. Review the section on cutting bias strips before you begin.

Making a Handle

Press under 1 cm (⅜ in) on the long edges, then press lengthways in half, matching the pressed edges. Stitch close to both pressed edges.

> **Tip:** Make sure that you stitch both edges of the handle in the same direction so that the fabric doesn't drag.

Stitching Ends

Attach the ends of a handle or tie to an item by stitching in all directions in a cross formation within a stitched square. Not only will the stitching anchor the handle or tie securely but the cross formation looks attractive too.

1 Press under 1 cm (⅜ in) on the ends of the handle or tie. Snip diagonally across the corners.

2 Pin the end of the handle or tie to the item. Stitch close to the edges and then across the handle or tie, forming a square. Stitch a cross formation in the centre of the square.

Making a Rouleau

A narrow tube of bias-cut fabric is called a rouleau, and can be used to make button loops and decorative loops and ties; being bias cut, the rouleau bends easily. When calculating the width to cut the bias strip, double the required width and then add two 6 mm (¼ in) seam allowances. Refer to the **Cutting Bias Strips technique** on page 56. When making button loops, cut bias strips 2.5 cm (1 in) wide.

1 Fold a bias strip of fabric lengthways in half with right sides facing. Stitch the long edges, taking a 6 mm (¼ in) seam allowance. If using a 2.5 cm (1 in) wide or narrower bias strip, trim the seam allowance.

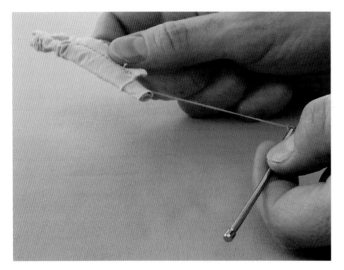

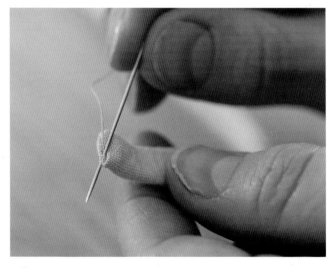

2 To turn right side out, fasten a bodkin to one end of the tube with a short length of thread (see page 12). Ease the bodkin through the tube and it will pull the rouleau right side out. Alternatively, slip a rouleau turner into the tube (see page 12), hook the end onto the end of the tube and pull through. If the rouleau has wrinkled, steam by holding a steam iron just above the wrinkles. The rouleau may stretch when being turned right side out, so measure it and trim it to the length you require, if necessary.

3 If necessary, neaten the end of the rouleau by poking the raw end inside the tube and then slipstitching the end closed (see page 25).

Portable doorstop

Besides its practical purpose, this doorstop makes a strong visual statement with the use of vibrant patterned fabric. The handle at the top enables it to be moved withe ease from place to place where needed. Rice is used here to provide a weighty filling, but you could use sand or dried beans.

YOU WILL NEED

- 30 cm (⅓ yd) of 137 cm (54 in) wide red patterned soft furnishing fabric
- 12.5 x 8 cm (5 x 3¼ in) rectangle of iron-on medium interfacing
- 1.75 kg (3¾ lb) uncooked rice

CUTTING OUT

Refer to the template on page 139 to cut from red patterned soft furnishing fabric:
- Four doorstop gussets
- One 12.5 x 8 cm (5 x 3¼ in) rectangle for the handle
- One 11 cm (4⅜ in) square for the top
- One 15 cm (5⅞ in) square for the base

Tip: Add some dried lavender to the filling to gently scent the room.

1 Press the interfacing to the wrong side of the handle. Follow the **Making a Handle technique** on page 76 to make the handle. Pin the handle across the centre of the right side of the doorstop top, matching the raw edges. Stitch the handle in place 6 mm (¼ in) inside the raw edges. Taking a 1 cm (⅜ in) seam allowance, follow the **Turning Gusset Corners technique** on page 40 to stitch the gussets together along the long slanted edges and then to stitch the gussets to the doorstop top and base, leaving a 10 cm (4 in) gap in one edge of the base to turn through.

2 Turn the doorstop right side out. To define the gusset seams, fold along one gusset seam with the wrong sides facing. Topstitch 5 mm (¼ in) from the folded edge, starting and finishing 5 mm (¼ in) from the top and base. Repeat on the other gusset seams. Follow Steps 5–6 of the **Making a Filled Shape technique** on page 131 to fill the doorstop with rice.

Buttonholes, loops and buttons

As a general rule, to judge where to place buttons that are to be fastened through buttonholes, measure the diameter of the button and place the centre of the button three-quarters of the diameter measurement in from the finished edge of the fabric. For example, place the centre of a 2 cm (¾ in) diameter button 1.5 cm (⅝ in) in from the finished edge of the fabric, then mark the position with a pin.

Making a Buttonhole
The length of the buttonhole should equal the diameter of the button plus its height plus 3 mm (⅛ in). This measurement allows for stitches at each end of the buttonhole.

For a horizontal buttonhole, use a fine pencil or an air-erasable pen to draw a line the length of the buttonhole starting 3 mm (⅛ in) beyond the button position. For a vertical buttonhole, draw a line the length of the buttonhole parallel with finished edge of the fabric, with the button position at the centre. Make the buttonhole on the line using a buttonhole foot on your sewing machine. Cut the buttonhole open with a sharp pair of embroidery scissors.

Attaching a Button Loop
Follow the **Making a Rouleau technique** on page 77 to make a button loop. If making loops for a number of buttons, make a continuous rouleau, then cut it into individual lengths.

To judge the length to cut the loop, pin one end of the rouleau to the seam line, matching the raw end of the rouleau to the raw edge of the seam allowance. Place the centre of a button 3 mm (⅛ in) in from the seam line. Wrap the rouleau smoothly around the button and pin to the seam line. Cut off the excess rouleau level with the raw edge. Remove the button and tack (baste) the ends of the loop in place, with the loop seam facing inwards.

Covering a Self-Cover Button

1 Use the manufacturer's template to cut a circle of fabric for the size of button. Run a gathering thread by hand just inside the circumference of the circle. Place the button face down on the wrong side, then pull up the gathers to enclose the button.

2 Fasten the ends of the gathering thread and adjust the gathers evenly. Press the washer over the underside of the button to secure the fabric in place.

Sewing Buttons

Buttons that have a shank underneath allow the button to rest on top of the buttonhole or loop without squashing the fabric. Sew-through buttons have a flat back, but can have a thread shank added, as follows.

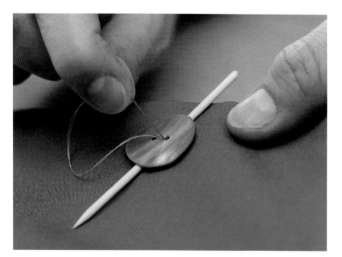

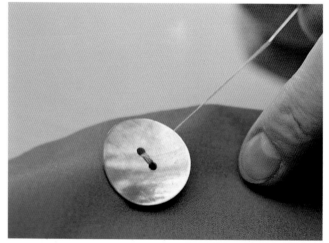

1 Anchor a double length of thread at the button position, then bring the thread up through a sew-through button. Place the button in position with a cocktail stick (toothpick) slipped underneath. Sew the button to the fabric, taking the thread over the stick, with about six stitches.

2 Pull out the cocktail stick (toothpick) and lift the button away from the fabric so that the stitches are taut. Wind the thread around the stitches to create a shank. Fasten the thread securely on the wrong side of the fabric.

Button-fastened cushion

This distinctive cushion is simple to make using the **Envelope Opening technique** on pages 68–69 to fasten the cushion with matching fabric-covered buttons. Combining two soft furnishing fabrics that link in terms of colour yet contrast in tone and pattern makes for a dynamic yet harmonious result. Alternatively, you could use two wildly contrasting fabrics.

YOU WILL NEED

- 40 cm (½ yd) of 137 cm (54 in) wide pink on cream patterned soft furnishing fabric
- 40 cm (½ yd) of 137 cm (54 in) wide pink patterned soft furnishing fabric
- Three 29 mm (1¼ in) self-cover buttons
- 30 cm (12 in) square cushion pad

CUTTING OUT

From pink on cream patterned soft furnishing fabric, cut:

- Two 33 x 14 cm (13 x 5½ in) rectangles for the flap

From pink patterned soft furnishing fabric, cut:

- Two 33 cm (13¼ in) squares for the back and front

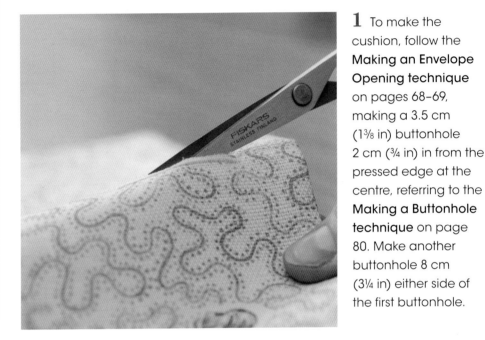

1 To make the cushion, follow the **Making an Envelope Opening technique** on pages 68–69, making a 3.5 cm (1⅜ in) buttonhole 2 cm (¾ in) in from the pressed edge at the centre, referring to the **Making a Buttonhole technique** on page 80. Make another buttonhole 8 cm (3¼ in) either side of the first buttonhole.

2 Mark the position of the buttons under the buttonholes. Follow the **Covering a Self-Cover Button technique** on page 81 to cover the three buttons with offcuts of pink patterned soft furnishing fabric. Sew the buttons to the front. Insert the cushion pad and fasten the buttons.

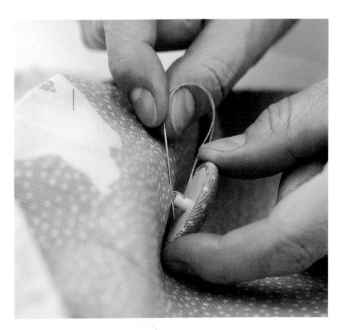

Casings

A drawstring bag (using a casing) has many different uses and can be made in a wide range of sizes. Tiny bags about 14 cm (5½ in) wide are just the thing for protecting precious jewellery or to present a special gift, while ones at least 40 cm (16 in) wide are perfect for laundry or storing toys.

Making a Casing

The following instructions are for a bag that has a 2 cm (¾ in) wide casing with a 2 cm (¾ in) wide allowance above, which will gather into a frill when the drawstrings are pulled. Start by cutting two pieces of fabric for the front and back of the bag to the size you want, adding a 1.5 cm (⅝ in) seam allowance to the side and lower edges, and a 6.5 cm (2½ in) allowance to the upper edge.

1 Neaten the side and lower edges with a zigzag stitch (see the **Neatening Seams technique**, page 36). With right sides facing and taking a 1.5 cm (⅝ in) seam allowance, stitch the side and lower edges, leaving a 2 cm (¾ in) gap 8.5 cm (3⅜ in) below the upper edge. Press the seams open.

2 Press under 1 cm (⅜ in) on the upper edge and stitch in place.

> **Tip:** If your bag is small, you may find it easier to stitch it with the bed of your sewing machine removed.

3 Press the upper edge inside the bag for 5.5 cm (2¼ in). Turn the bag right side out.

4 On the right side, stitch 2 cm (¾ in) and then 4 cm (1½ in) below the upper pressed edge to form the channel.

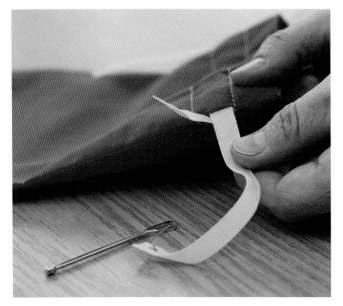

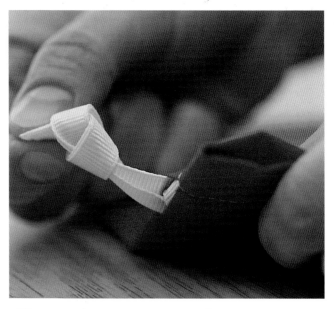

5 Cut two drawstrings from ribbon or cord each measuring three times the width of the bag. Use a bodkin (see page 12) to thread one drawstring through the channel, entering and emerging through the same gap. Repeat with the other drawstring through the other gap.

6 Knot the ends of the drawstrings together 5 cm (2 in) above the ends.

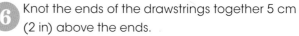

YOU WILL NEED

- 20 cm (¼ yd) of 90 cm (36 in) wide iron-on medium interfacing
- 20 cm (8 in) square of pink striped cotton fabric
- 20 cm (8 in) square of green patterned cotton fabric
- 20 cm (8 in) square of orange spotted cotton fabric
- 50 cm (½ yd) of 137 cm (54 in) wide light blue spotted soft furnishing fabric
- 2.1 m (2⅓ yd) of thick piping cord
- Sticky tape

CUTTING OUT

Press interfacing to the wrong side of the cotton fabrics. Use the template on page 141 to cut:
- Six bunting triangles

From light blue spotted soft furnishing fabric, cut:
- Two 38 x 16 cm (15 x 6¼ in) rectangles for the band
- Two 40 x 38 cm (15¾ x 15 in) rectangles for the bag

Toy sack

This jaunty nautical-styled toy sack is sure to inspire the children to engage in some enthusiastic tidying up of their playthings. The sack is decked with a colourful row of bunting—another opportunity to plunder your stash of offcuts—and fastens with cord drawstrings.

1 With right sides facing up, pin a pink striped, green patterned and orange spotted bunting triangle in a row to each band—match the straight edges of the triangles to the long upper edges of the bands and butt the short edges of the triangles together 1.5 cm (⅝ in) inside the short edges of the bands. Tack (baste) in place.

2 With right sides facing and taking a 1.5 cm (⅝ in) seam allowance, stitch each tacked (basted) edge of a band to one short edge of a bag. Neaten the seam with a zigzag stitch (see the **Neatening Seams technique**, page 36). Press the seam towards the bag. On the right side, topstitch 7.5 mm (⁵⁄₁₆ in) above the seam. Follow Steps 1–4 of the **Making a Casing technique** on pages 84–85 to make the bag and casing.

3 To stop the cord unravelling, bind sticky tape around the centre and both ends of the cord, then cut the cord in half. Follow Steps 5–6 of the **Making a Casing technique** on pages 84–85 to thread and knot the cord drawstrings. Pull off the tapes at the ends of the cords. Unravel and separate the strands of the cord ends below the knots. Moisten the strands to remove the kinks and then trim the ends level.

YOU WILL NEED

- 1.3 m (1½ yd) of 112 cm (44 in) olive green patterned cotton fabric
- 30 cm (⅓ yd) of 112 cm (44 in) wide olive green embroidery anglaise cotton fabric
- 1.3 m (1½ yd) of 90 cm (36 in) wide iron-on medium interfacing

CUTTING OUT

Follow the **Making a Border Pattern technique** on page 88 to make a pattern for the runner.

From olive green patterned cotton fabric and iron-on medium interfacing, cut:
- Two long borders
- Two short borders

From olive green embroidery anglaise cotton fabric, cut:
- One 108 x 26 cm (42½ x 10¼ in) rectangle for the centre panel

Mitred border runner

Smarten up your dinner table with this sophisticated runner. Provided it is cut with accuracy, the mitred border is easy to stitch and gives a crisp, tailored look. The runner shown here measures 120 x 38 cm (47¼ x 15 in) overall with 7 cm (2¾ in) deep borders, but it can be made to any size, to suit your table's dimensions.

1 Press the interfacing to the wrong side of the patterned borders.

2 Follow the **Making a Border Pattern** and **Applying a Border techniques** on pages 88–89 to make the runner.

Scallops

The scallop is a classic shape that you will frequently come across in soft furnishings, whether as an edging for table linen or in a curtain heading, and it always looks effective. Make a semicircle or a circle of thin card to use as a template for the scallops, and it can be used again and again.

Making a Scallop Heading

A scallop heading can be used to make traditional café-style curtains. The upper edge of the fabric is folded over to form a facing and the scallops are stitched through both thicknesses. The following instructions are for 10 cm (4 in) diameter scallops, which is a popular size. Add 10 cm (4 in) to the upper edge for a facing for 10 cm (4 in) diameter scallops, and allow one and a half widths of fabric for a café curtain—fabric widths can be joined using the **Sewing a Flat Felled Seam technique** on page 29. Before making the scallops, make a plain hem at each side of the curtain (see page 46).

1 Press under 5 mm (¼ in) on the upper edge and stitch in place to hem the facing. Fold the facing to the right side for 9.5 cm (3¾ in). Lay the fabric out flat and mark the centre of the upper edge with a pin on the fold. Cut a semicircle of card to use as a template for the scallops. Place the template 1 cm (⅜ in) from the centre pin, matching the straight edge of the template to the fold. Mark the edges of the template with a pin on the fold. Move the template along the facing fold, leaving a 2 cm (¾ in) gap between the scallops, marking the edges with pins as before. Place the last scallop about 2 cm (¾ in) inside the side hem, adjusting the size of the gaps between the scallops if necessary.

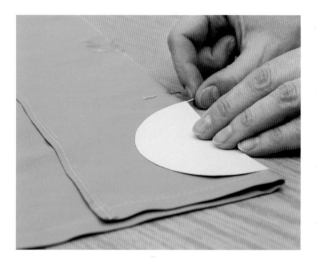

2 Replace the template in the first position and draw around the curves with an-air-erasable pen. Draw all the scallops at the pinned positions. Repeat to draw the scallops on the other half of the facing. Stitch along the drawn lines.

3 Trim the scallops, leaving a 6 mm (¼ in) seam allowance. Clip the corners and snip the curves. Turn right side out and press. Slipstitch the hemmed side edges of the facing to the side hems of the curtains (see page 25).

Making a Scallop Edging

You can enhance a throw, place mat or napkin with a decorative scallop edging. The edge can be a double layer of fabric that is stitched and 'bagged out' or applied to a single layer of fabric with a close zigzag stitch, such as to outline a napkin. The zigzag stitching can be reinforced with tear-away stabilizer (see page 17).

Draw the item to which you want to add scallops on a piece of paper. Divide the edge to be scalloped equally, which will equate to the diameter of each scallop. If the scallops continue around the item, cut a circle of card to the diameter required, then divide into quarters. If scallops are on one edge only, cut a semicircle to the diameter required.

1 Place the circle template on one corner, matching the quarter lines to the outline. Draw around the outer three-quarters of the circle. Repeat on each corner. Move the template along the outline and draw around the outer edge of the circle.

2 Place the straight edge of the semicircle template on the outline, matching the centres. Draw around the semicircle. Move the template along the outline and draw around the curves. Cut out the pattern.

3 Pin two layers of fabric together with right sides facing for a straight-stitched item that will be turned to the right side; use one layer of fabric for a zigzag edging. Draw around the pattern on the fabric with an air-erasable pen. Stitch along the outline, remembering to leave a gap if you need to turn the item through. Trim the scallops leaving a 6 mm (¼ in) seam allowance on an item to be turned, clip the corners and snip the curves, then turn right side out. Follow the instructions for the **Zigzag Edging technique** on pages 36–37.

Café curtain

YOU WILL NEED

- 112 cm (44 in) wide pink on aqua patterned cotton fabric (quantity depends on size of curtain)
- 10 cm (4 in) semicircle of card
- Curtain rings with clips or sew-on curtain rings (quantity depends on size of curtain)

CUTTING OUT

Slip a curtain ring with a clip or a sew-on curtain ring onto the curtain rod. Measure the drop of the curtain from the top of the opening of the clip or the bottom of a sew-on curtain ring to sill level. Measure the width of rod.

From pink on aqua patterned cotton fabric, cut:

- The curtain drop plus a 10 cm (4 in) facing and a 10 cm (4 in) hem x one and a half times the width plus 5 cm (2 in) for side hems

The ever-popular café curtain makes a pretty addition to a kitchen window, and instantly brings atmosphere to the interior. It has the added benefit of offering privacy while allowing you to see out at the same time. Attach the scalloped heading to an attractive curtain rod with curtain rings. If you need to join fabric widths, refer to the **Sewing a Flat Felled Seam technique** on page 29.

1 Press under 1 cm (³⁄₈ in) and then 1.5 cm (⁵⁄₈ in) on the side edges. To hem the side edges, stitch close to the inner pressed edges or slipstitch in place (see page 25). Follow the **Making a Scallop Heading technique** on page 92 to make the curtain, then follow the **Making a Curtain Hem technique** on page 47 to hem the lower edge.

2 Fix the clip of a curtain ring onto the curtain or sew a sew-on curtain ring to the top of the curtain between the scallops. Slip the rings onto your chosen curtain rod.

Trimmings and fringing

Ribbon can only be applied in straight lines unless it is gathered, when it can then be used for curves, whereas most woven braids and ric-rac can be applied to gentle curves as well as straight lines. To pin ribbon or braid in a straight line, either draw a line with an air-erasable pen to line it up against or butt the trimming up against a ruler. Ric-rac is applied by stitching along its centre.

Applying Ribbon

Pin the ribbon to the fabric. Stitch close to one edge of the ribbon, then stitch close to the other edge. Always stitch both ribbon edges in the same direction, otherwise the ribbon will drag and wrinkle.

Turning Ribbon Corners

1 Starting 1 cm (⅜ in) beyond one corner, pin the ribbon in a straight line to form one edge of the square or rectangle. Starting 1 cm (⅜ in) from the end, stitch close to the outer edge of the ribbon as far as the next corner. At the end of the stitching, fold the ribbon back on itself with right sides facing.

2 Lift the ribbon and fold it diagonally at the corner, then pin the ribbon along the next adjacent edge. Tack (baste) the mitred corner in place. Repeat at the next corner and continue pinning the ribbon until you reach the first corner.

3 Fold the ribbon under diagonally at the first corner. Stitch close to the inner edges of the ribbon, then cut off the excess ribbon under the folded corner. Tack (baste) the corner in place. Stitch close to the remaining outer edges of the ribbon.

Fringing

A loosely woven fabric is best for fringing. Woven stripes are very effective, as the adjacent edges will look quite different to each other and the main body of the fabric.

Knotting a Fringe

The fringe must be at least 7.5 cm (3 in) deep to make a knotted edge. The fringe can be trimmed with scissors after knotting if you wish.

Carefully cut the fabric along the grainlines. Use a long needle to gently pull away the threads from one edge. To prevent tangling, work on one thread at a time.

After fringing, divide the edge of the fabric into equal sections, for example 2 cm (¾ in) apart, and mark each division with a pin. Knot each section just below the fabric.

Wavy line throw

Add an understated decorative touch to a classic chenille throw by couching thick embroidery yarn or knitting wool using a zigzag stitch on your sewing machine. It's a wonderfully simple, speedy way to add an accent of colour to the throw. Alternatively, couch the yarn to a ready-made throw.

1 Set the sewing machine to a 3 mm (⅛ in) wide and 3 mm (⅛ in) long zigzag stitch. Thread the machine with sewing thread to match the embroidery yarn on top and to match the throw in the bobbin. Lay the embroidery yarn on the right side of the throw at least 17 cm (6¾ in) in from and parallel with one short edge. Reverse stitch to anchor the yarn at one long edge, then zigzag stitch over the yarn with the yarn centred. Move the yarn in gentle curves as you zigzag stitch to create a wavy line. Cut off the excess yarn level with the long edge of the throw and reverse stitch to secure it. Repeat to apply three wavy rows of yarn approximately 3 cm (1¼ in) apart at the short edges of the throw.

2 Follow the **Fringing technique** on page 97 to fringe the short edges for 11 cm (4¼ in). Follow Step 1 of the **Making a Plain Hem technique** on page 46 to hem the long edges—the depth of the hem should be 1.5 cm (⅝ in). Stitch close to the inner pressed edges. Follow the **Knotting a Fringe technique** on page 97 to knot the fringe at both short edges of the throw.

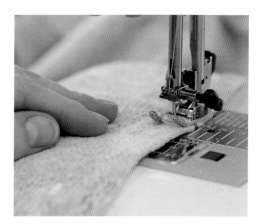

Ribbon-trimmed sheet

The upper edge of a sheet is often visible on the bed, so why not add a few rows of ribbon to coordinate it with your bedroom décor? It's such a simple treatment, but it will bring a unique designer style to your bedding. The ribbon can be added to a ready-made sheet for a near-instant makeover, or follow the steps below to a make a sheet from scratch.

YOU WILL NEED

For a single sheet:

■ 2.8 m (3¼ yd) of 240 cm (94 in) wide lilac cotton sheeting

■ 1.9 m (2¼ yd) of 1 cm (⅜ in) wide purple/black gingham ribbon

■ 1.9 m (2¼ yd) of 2.5 cm (1 in) wide wine taffeta ribbon

For a double sheet:

■ 2.8 m (3¼ yd) of 240 cm (94 in) wide lilac cotton sheeting

■ 2.4 m (2¾ yd) of 1 cm (⅜ in) wide purple/black gingham ribbon

■ 2.4 m (2¾ yd) of 2.5 cm (1 in) wide wine taffeta ribbon

CUTTING OUT

From lilac cotton sheeting, cut:

■ One 272 x 185 cm (107 x 73 in) rectangle for a single sheet

From lilac cotton sheeting, cut:

■ One 272 x 235 cm (107 x 92½ in) rectangle for a double sheet

1 Refer to the **Applying Ribbon technique** on page 96 to pin and stitch the purple/black gingham ribbon 12 cm (4¾ in) below the short top edge of the sheet on the right side. Pin and stitch the wine taffeta ribbon 2.5 cm (1 in) below the gingham ribbon.

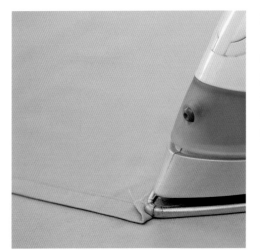

2 Press under 1 cm (⅜ in) and then 1.5 cm (⅝ in) on the long side edges of the sheet. Stitch close to the inner pressed edges. Press under 1 cm (⅜ in) on the short top and bottom edges. Open out the corners, then press under diagonally.

3 Press under 5 cm (2 in) on the top and bottom edges, then stitch close to the inner pressed edges.

Tip: To apply ribbon to a ready-made sheet, follow Step 1, turning under the ends of the ribbon to start and finish.

Ribbon-trimmed sheet **101**

CUTTING OUT

- 12 cm (4¾ in) square for each coaster

Fringed coasters

Traditional tea towels are often woven in stripes in wonderful colour combinations, and they are ideal candidates for fringing and making into vibrant coasters. This is a fun project for a home sewing beginner or those who haven't tried the zigzag stitch function on their sewing machine before. Take care to cut the fabric carefully along the grain lines.

1 Set the sewing machine to a 3 mm (⅛ in) wide and 1 mm (¹⁄₁₆ in) long zigzag stitch. Use a ruler and sharp pencil or air-erasable pen to draw a border on the right side of the coaster 1.5 cm (⅝ in) from the cut edges. Leaving a trailing length of top and bobbin thread to start on one drawn line, zigzag stitch along the lines. When you reach each corner, keep the needle in the outer edge of the zigzagging while you lift the presser foot. Pivot the coaster so that the presser foot is facing along the next line.

2 Continue along all the edges of the drawn square. Follow Step 3 of the **Zigzag Edging technique** on page 37 to secure the stitching. Cut off the excess threads. Follow the **Fringing technique** on page 97 to fringe the coasters as far as the zigzag stitching.

Gathering and frills

A frill is a gathered strip of fabric that can be used on cushions and curtains. The frill can be stitched along its centre on top of the main fabric to make a double frill or stitched in a seam allowance to make a single frill. A frill can also be made from ribbon, which doesn't need hemming. Cut the frill twice the length of the area it is to be applied to, except for very fine fabrics such as voile, chiffon and muslin where you should cut it two and a half times as long. Refer to the **Sewing a Flat Felled Seam technique** on page 29 if you need to join the frills.

Making a Single Frill

1 Cut the frill to the desired width plus 2 cm (¾ in) for the hem and seam allowance. Turn under 5 mm (¼ in) twice on one long edge and stitch in place to hem the frill. Also hem the ends of the frill if necessary. Press the hem. Divide the long raw edge of the frill and the edge of the main fabric into quarters, then insert a pin at right angles to the raw edges to mark each quarter. Use a contrast-coloured thread and the longest straight stitch on your sewing machine to stitch a gathering thread 5 mm (¼ in) from the raw edge of the frill. Don't reverse stitch at each end, but leave the thread ends trailing.

2 With right sides facing, pin the frill to the main fabric, matching the raw edges and divisions and ends of the frill to the edges of the main fabric. Pull up the gathering thread to gather the frill, adjusting the gathers evenly along the length. Pin or tack (baste) in place.

Making a Double Frill

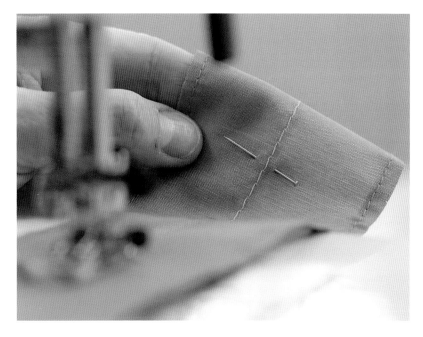

① Cut the frill to the desired width plus 2 cm (1 in) for hems. Turn under 5 mm (¼ in) twice on the long edges and stitch in place to hem the frill. Press the hems. Fold the frill lengthways in half with right sides facing and press lightly along the fold. Open out flat again. Fold the frill into quarters and insert a pin at right angles across the fold line to mark each quarter on the right side. Use a contrast-coloured thread and the longest straight stitch on your sewing machine to stitch a gathering thread 3 mm (⅛ in) from the fold line, starting and finishing at the end seam allowances. Don't reverse stitch at each end, but leave the thread ends trailing, stitching carefully over the pins.

② Use a water-soluble pen, air-erasable pen or sharp tailor's chalk and a ruler to draw a line on the right side of the background fabric where the centre of the frill will be applied. Divide the line into quarters and mark the divisions with the pen or chalk.

③ With right sides facing up, pin the frill to the background fabric, matching the fold line to the drawn line. Match the divisions and the ends of the frill to the raw edges of the background fabric. Pull the ends of the top gathering thread to gather the frill to fit, adjusting the gathers evenly along the length. Keep the gathers within the seam allowances at the ends of the frill. Pin or tack (baste) in place.

④ Set the sewing machine to a regular stitch length. Use sewing thread to match the frill to stitch along the centre of the frill. Remove the gathering thread and any tacking (basting).

Ruffle cushion

YOU WILL NEED

- 70 cm (¾ yd) of 137 cm (54 in) wide green plain cotton soft furnishing fabric
- 40 cm (16 in) zip (zipper)
- 45 x 35 cm (18 x 13¾ in) cushion pad

CUTTING OUT

From green plain cotton soft furnishing fabric, cut:

- One 96 x 20 cm (38 x 8 in) strip for the frill
- One 48 x 38 cm (19¼ x 15 in) rectangle for the front
- Two 48 x 20.5 cm (19¼ x 8⅛ in) rectangles for the back

This flamboyant cushion would add a lovely element of drama and decadence to a living room or bedroom. The bold frill across the front is simple to apply using the double frill technique. The frill would also look good in a contrasting fabric to the cushion, if you prefer.

1 Draw a line across the centre of the front parallel with the long edges on the right side using an air-erasable pen, water-soluble pen or sharp tailor's chalk. Follow the **Making a Double Frill technique** on pages 104–105 to stitch the frill to the front. Tack (baste) the ends of the frill to the short edges of the front, matching the raw edges.

2 With right sides facing, place the backs together, matching the raw edges. Follow the **Inserting a Zip (Zipper) technique** on pages 72–73 to sew the zip (zipper) into one long edge so that it will sit along the centre of the cushion. With right sides facing, pin the front and back together. Stitch the outer edges, taking a 1.5 cm (⅝ in) seam allowance. Clip the corners and turn the cushion right side out. Insert the cushion pad and fasten the zip (zipper).

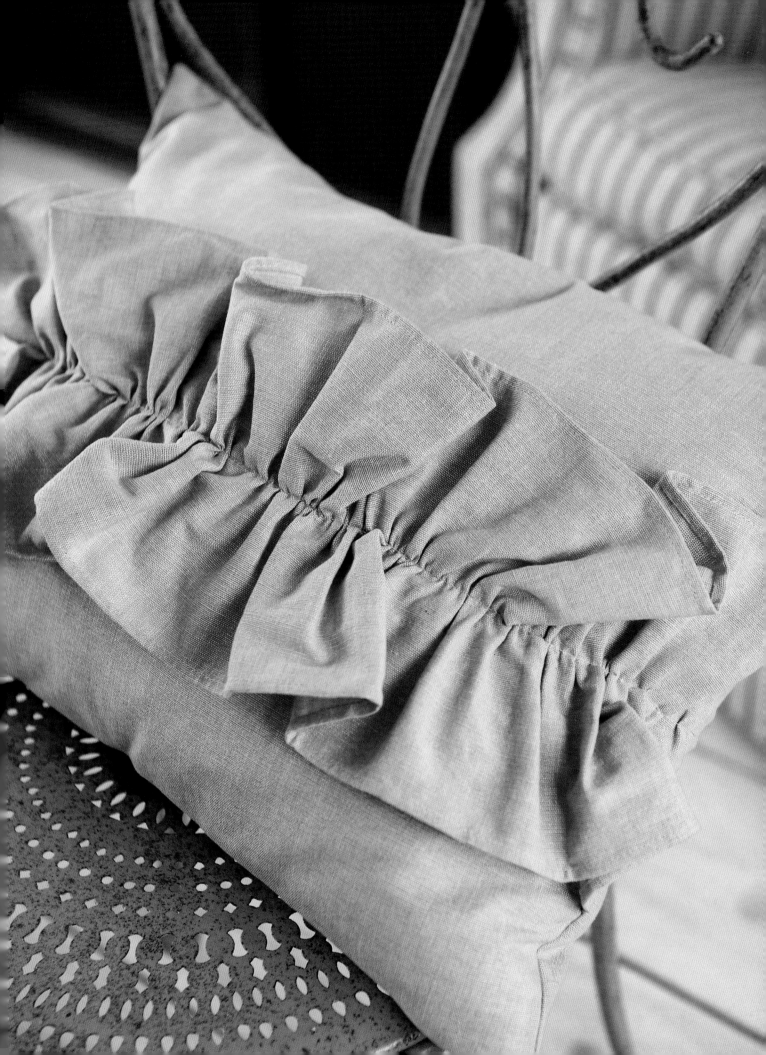

Pleats

Pleats are a method of adding fullness by folding a piece of fabric back on itself. Knife pleats have folds that lay in one direction, while inverted box pleats have two pleats facing each other that meet at the centre. A box pleat is made in exactly the same way as an inverted box pleat, but on the other side of the fabric. For best results, make pleats on the straight grain.

Making a Knife Pleat

Allow twice the required depth of the pleat when making patterns and cutting fabric. For example, for a 2.5 cm (1 in) deep pleat, add 5 cm (2 in) to the pattern.

1 If the pleat is to be loose and unstitched, make the hem first. Fold the fabric at the pleat position and press.

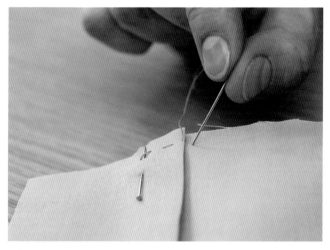

2 For a loose pleat, insert a pin level with the pressed edge to mark the depth of the pleat. Lay the pressed edge in the direction that the pleat is to fall and tack (baste) across the upper edge.

3 For a stitched pleat, match the pressed edge to the relevant marking on the needle plate of the sewing machine for the depth of the pleat. Stitch the pleat in place, keeping the pressed edge level with the needle plate marking. Lay the fabric flat on the ironing board and press the pleat in the direction required.

Making an Inverted Box Pleat

Make an inverted box pleat at the corner of seat covers and bed valances. Allow four times the required depth of the pleat when making patterns and cutting fabric. For example, for an inverted box pleat with a pair of 2.5 cm (1 in) deep pleats that meet at the centre, add 10 cm (4 in) to the pattern. Make the hem before making the pleat.

Measuring along from one end of the upper edge, mark the position of the inverted pleat with a pin. Measure twice the depth of each pleat from the pin and mark with a pin. Bring the pins to meet at the centre and tack (baste) upper edges. If the pleat is at a corner, snip the seam allowance at the centre of the pleat. Press the pleats with the edges butting together.

Making an Upholstered Inverted Box Pleat

Fold away the fullness of fabric neatly at the corners of an upholstered seat with an inverted box pleat. Using a staple gun makes the job very quick, clean and simple. Keep the fabric taut and smooth as you work.

1 After stapling the side edges of the fabric to the underside of the seat, pull the fabric over one corner of the seat and staple it to the underside.

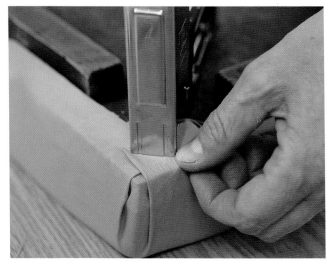

2 Fold under the fullness neatly either side of the corner and staple to the underside of the seat.

YOU WILL NEED

- 137 cm (54 in) wide pink chequered soft furnishing fabric (quantity depends on size of chair)
- 90 cm (36 in) wide iron-on medium loft fleece (quantity depends on size of chair)
- 90 cm (36 in) wide natural cotton fabric (quantity depends on size of chair)

CUTTING OUT

See Steps on page 112, from pink chequered soft furnishing fabric, cut:

- One seat
- One strip that is A + B + C + B + A plus 24 cm (10 in) for the inverted box pleats plus 16 cm (6½ in) for facings x the drop plus a 1 cm (⅜ in) seam allowance plus a 3.5 cm (1⅜ in) hem for the skirt. If necessary, join fabric to make the skirt with a flat felled seam (see page 29)
- Four 36 x 3.5 cm (14¼ x 1⅜ in) bias strips for ties

See Steps on page 112, from iron-on medium loft fleece and natural cotton fabric, cut:

- One seat, trimming 5 mm (¼ in) from the outer edges of the fleece

Chair seat cover

Soften the appearance of a hard-seated chair with a smart skirted seat cover. A layer of iron-on fleece adds some cushioning, and inverted box pleats at the front corners tailor the look. The cover fastens to the back rails of the chair with pretty ties.

1 To make the pattern, cut a piece of pattern or parcel paper larger than the seat. Place it on the seat with a weight on top to keep it in place. Fold the edges of the paper over the seat to define the shape. If necessary, snip the paper around the rails so that it lies flat. Mark the position of the outer rails at the back edge. Measure the depth of one back rail (A), one side edge of the seat (B) and the front edge of the seat (C). Remove the pattern. Draw along the folded edges and around the rails, then cut it out. Trace around the pattern onto another sheet of paper. Mark the outer rails, add a 1 cm (⅜ in) seam allowance to all edges and cut out the new pattern. Draw the grain line parallel with the centre of the cover. Label the pattern 'Seat'. Decide on the drop of the skirt, that is how long you want the skirt to be—the drop of this skirt is 20 cm (8 in).

2 Follow the **Making a Rouleau technique** on page 77 to make the ties, pressing the seams open before turning the ties right side out. Neaten one end of each tie and press the ties flat. Press the fleece centrally to the wrong side of the pink chequered seat. With right sides facing, tack (baste) the raw ends of two ties to the back edge on the right side of the pink chequered seat 1 cm (⅜ in) inside the back rail position.

3 Pin the seats together with right sides facing. Stitch the back edge, taking a 1 cm (⅜ in) seam allowance. Snip to any corners and clip corners and curves. Turn right side out and press. Tack (baste) the raw edges together.

4 Follow the **Making a Plain Hem technique** on page 46 to sew a 2.5 cm (1 in) deep hem on the lower edge of the skirt. Press under 1 cm (⅜ in) at the ends of the skirt, then press the pressed edge under diagonally at the lower edges. Stitch in place to hem the facings. Follow the **Making an Inverted Box Pleat technique** on page 109 to make a 3 cm (1¼ in) deep inverted box pleat 7 cm (2⅞ in) plus A and B from each end of the skirt.

5 With right sides facing and matching the raw edges, pin the skirt to the seat, matching the centre of the pleats to the corners. Fold back 7 cm (2⅞ in) at each end of the skirt to form the facings, enclosing the ends of the back edge of the seat, and pin in place. Stitch the raw edges, taking a 1 cm (⅜ in) seam allowance and pivoting the seam at the front corners. Clip the corners. Neaten the seam with a zigzag stitch (see the **Neatening Seams technique** on page 36).

6 Turn the facings to the underside of the skirt and press a neat edge at each end of the skirt. Press the seam towards the skirt. Follow the **Stitching Ends technique** on page 76 to stitch the ends of the remaining ties to the wrong side of the facing and skirt 6 mm (¼ in) below the seam and 1.5 cm (⅝ in) in from the pressed edge.

Upholstered footstool

The humble footstool is a frequently neglected yet highly practical item. Simply replace its care-worn cover with a lively patterned fabric and it will seem like a new piece of furniture. A staple gun is a useful tool to make the task quick and easy to achieve.

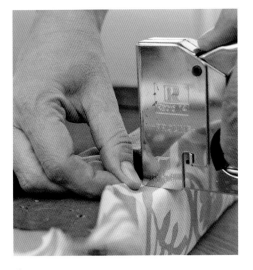 

1 Place the cover, wrong side up, on a flat surface. Place the seat face down on the centre of the cover. Lift one edge of the cover over the seat and staple it to the underside of the seat at the centre of the edge. Repeat on the opposite edge of the seat, pulling the fabric so that it lays smoothly over the seat on the right side. Repeat to staple the adjacent edges. Lift the seat to the right side to make sure that the fabric is taut and smooth. Remove and replace the staples if necessary. Working outwards from the centre of the edges, staple the cover to the underside of the seat, keeping the fabric taut and stopping about 7.5 cm (3 in) from the corners.

2 Follow the **Making an Upholstered Inverted Box Pleat technique** on page 109 to staple the fabric neatly at the corners. Replace the seat in the stool.

Tip: If you are short of fabric, you can stitch bands of fabric together to make one piece to use to upholster a stool—that way you can feature a small element of a fabric that occurs elsewhere in the room.

YOU WILL NEED

- 112 cm (44 in) or 137 cm (54 in) wide turquoise spotted cotton fabric (quantity depends on size of tablecloth)
- White topstitching thread

CUTTING OUT

From turquoise spotted cotton fabric, cut:

- A rectangle or square to the tablecloth size required with 10.5 cm (4 in) added to all edges for the tablecloth

> **Tip:** To make a large tablecloth, you can join fabric widths following the **Sewing a Flat Felled Seam technique** on page 29.

Pleated tablecloth

Add decorative detailing to a classic tablecloth to create a cloth with a border of deep knife pleats, making for an interesting intersection at the corners. Choose a plain fabric or one with a simple pattern in muted colours to show off the pleats. Topstitching the pleats in contrast-coloured thread gives them extra definition.

1 Fold two opposite edges of the fabric with wrong sides facing 12.5 cm (5 in) from the raw edges. Press in place. Turn the tablecloth to the right side. Follow Step 3 of the **Making a Knife Pleat technique** on page 108 to make 2 cm (¾ in) deep pleats using white topstitching thread as the top thread. Press the pleats towards the raw edges.

2 To make the next pleat, fold and press the tablecloth 4.5 cm (1¾ in) in from the stitched pleats. Stitch and press in place as before.

3 Repeat Steps 1–2 to make two pleats on the other edges of the tablecloth in the same way. Follow the **Making a Plain Hem technique** on page 46 to make a 1.5 cm (⅝ in) deep hem on all the edges, using ordinary sewing thread.

Curtains and linings

Curtains are probably the largest and most costly item you will make. Don't be daunted, measuring is the most difficult part. Although large to handle, stitching the curtains is a straightforward process.

Measuring Up

If possible, have the curtain fittings in place before measuring for fabric. If this is not possible, lightly mark their intended position on the wall or window frame. Slip a few rings or hooks onto a curtain track or pole. For headings on a track, measure the intended drop (length) from the top of the track. For curtains hanging from rings, measure from the bottom of the ring. Decide on the length the curtain is to be, then add 3 cm (1¼ in) to the upper edge and a 10 cm (4 in) hem.

Measure the width of the track or pole with a steel tape or long ruler. For overlapping tracks in two halves, add the length of the overlap. Multiply this measurement by one and a half to three times for a gathered heading or by two to two and a half times for a pencil pleat or eyelet heading. Add a 2.5 cm (1 in) hem at each side for an unlined curtain and a 4 cm (1½ in) hem either side for lined curtains.

Fabric and Lining Widths

Unless a window is very narrow, widths of fabric must be joined to make curtains. Divide the total width measurement by the width of your chosen fabric to calculate the number of fabric widths required, then round up the fabric widths to the largest amount (there will be a 1.5 cm (⅝ in) seam on each edge). Refer to the **Matching Patterned Fabrics technique** on page 23 for how to match up pattern repeats and join widths. If you have an uneven number of fabric widths and there will be a pair of curtains at a window, cut one width lengthways in half and place it at the outer edge of the curtains. For lined curtains, the same amount of lining is needed as for curtain fabric minus the hem; there is no need to allow extra for matching patterns and pattern repeats. Cut the selvedges off the cutain and lining widths, otherwise the seams may pucker.

Using Interlining

A layer of interlining within a lined curtain provides heat and noise insulation as well as giving body to the curtain. Cut interlining to the drop measurement x the curtain width plus a 4 cm (1½ in) hem at each side.

To join widths, butt the edges together and join with a large, wide **zigzag stitch** (see page 36) or by hand with a **herringbone stitch** (see page 25). Try not to stretch the interlining when joining. Join curtain and lining widths with flat seams pressed open. Lay the curtain out flat wrong side up. Lay interlining smoothly on top 3 cm (1¼ in) below the upper edge. Fold one half of the interlining back on itself, aligning the fabric grains. Follow Step 3 onwards of the **Making a Lined Curtain technique** on page 120 to lock in interlining and complete the curtain.

Making a Lined Curtain

After measuring and cutting out the curtains and lining, join the curtain widths and lining widths with flat seams pressed open.

1 Press 4 cm (1½ in) to the wrong side on the side edges. Secure in place with a herringbone stitch (see page 25). Follow the **Making a Curtain Hem technique** on page 47 to make a hem on the lower edge. If you prefer, make the curtain hem once the curtain is hung.

2 Press under 1.5 cm (⅝ in) and then 3.5 cm (1⅜ in) on the lower edge of the lining. Stitch close to the inner pressed edge to hem the lining. Lay the curtain out flat wrong side up on a large table or on the floor. Place the lining on top with wrong sides facing and the lower edge 5 cm (2 in) above the lower edge of a hemmed curtain or 15 cm (6 in) above the lower edge of an unhemmed curtain. Pin the layers together along the centre, parallel with the side edges. Fold one half of the lining back on itself, aligning the fabric grains and top edges.

 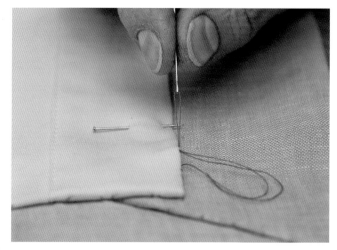

3 To join the lining to the curtain, starting 22.5 cm (9 in) above the lower edge of the curtain, use a long double length of thread to pick up two threads of the lining and curtain fabric. Draw the thread around the needle and pull through. Leave a gap of about 10 cm (4 in) and repeat, catching the curtain and lining together along the length—keep the thread loose so that it doesn't pull at the fabric. Join the layers at 40 cm (16 in) intervals across the curtain. This is known as locking in. When locking seams together, sew through the seam allowance and not the surface of the curtain and lining.

4 Trim the side edges of the lining level with the curtain, then turn under 3 cm (1¼ in). Pin and then slipstitch in place (see page 25), taking care not to sew through to the front of the curtain. Slipstitch each end of the lower hem for 4 cm (1½ in). If making the curtain hem later, leave about 22.5 cm (9 in) of the side edges unsewn, then finish once the lower hem is sewn. See pages 126–127 to make the curtain heading.

Making an Unlined Curtain

After measuring and cutting out the curtains, join the widths with flat felled seams (see page 29).

Press under 1 cm (⅜ in) and then 1.5 cm (⅝ in) on the long side edges. Slipstitch (see page 25) or machine stitch close to the inner pressed edges. Follow the **Making a Curtain Hem technique** on page 47 to make a hem on the lower edge. See pages 126–127 to make the curtain heading.

Horizontal border eyelet curtain

The chunky chrome eyelets on this elegant curtain give the curtain heading a bold, contemporary look. Adding a horizontal border at the upper edge of the curtain draws the eye to the smart eyelets, but it's also an ingenious solution for adding length to the curtains if you are short of fabric.

1 If necessary, join the fabric and lining widths following the **Sewing a Flat Felled Seam technique** on page 28. With right sides facing, stitch the band to the upper edge of the curtain, taking a 1.5 cm (⅝ in) seam allowance. Press the seam open. Follow the **Making a Lined Curtain technique** on pages 119–120 to make and line the curtain. Follow Step 1 of the **Making a Curtain Heading technique** on page 126 to prepare the heading; if your fabric is particularly thick, trim the pressed under edge to 1.5 cm (⅝ in) to make it easier to fix the eyelets.

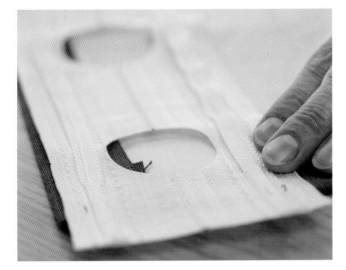

2 Lay the curtain out flat wrong side up. Place the eyelet tape on top. The tape is marked at regular intervals with a coloured, usually green marker. Adjust the tape so that the markers match the side edges of the curtain. If they don't match exactly, adjust the tape to ensure that the markers are an equal distance within the side edges of the curtain. Follow Steps 2–3 of the **Making a Curtain Heading technique** on page 126 to apply the tape to the curtain.

3 Carefully cut away the band and lining within the circles of the tape with a sharp pair of embroidery scissors. Place the half of the ring with spikes inside over one circle on the front of the band. Slip the other half underneath and clip the rings together, enclosing the raw edges of the circle. Fix all the rings in place.

4 Draw up the cords to pull the curtain up to the width required. Knot the free ends of the cords together, but don't cut them off. Adjust the curtain heading evenly. Follow Steps 5–6 of the **Making a Curtain Heading technique** on page 127 to finish the curtain.

Vertical border curtain

Adding a border to a curtain is a simple way of echoing other textiles in the room or introducing a refreshing contrast to an otherwise plain décor. A thin band of checked gingham ribbon cleverly hides the border seam between the main curtain fabric and the contrasting band.

YOU WILL NEED

- 137 cm (54 in) wide grey patterned soft furnishing fabric (quantity depends on size of curtain)
- 137 cm (54 in) wide pale olive green patterned soft furnishing fabric (quantity depends on size of curtain)
- 1.5 cm (⅝ in) wide grey gingham ribbon (quantity depends on size of curtain)
- 137 cm (54 in) wide natural curtain lining (quantity depends on size of curtain)
- Twice the curtain width plus 4 cm (1½ in) of 7.5 cm (3 in) wide pencil pleat curtain tape

CUTTING OUT

Measure the drop and width of the curtain—see the **Measuring and Fabric and Lining Widths technique** on page 118.

From grey patterned soft furnishing fabric, cut:

- The curtain drop plus 13 cm (5¼ in) x 22.5 cm (8⅞ in) for the band

From pale olive green patterned soft furnishing fabric, cut:

- The curtain drop plus 13 cm (5¼ in) x twice the curtain width less 11.5 cm (4⅝ in) for the curtain

From natural curtain lining, cut:

- The curtain drop plus 3 cm (1¼ in) x twice the curtain width plus 8 cm (3 in) for side hems for the lining

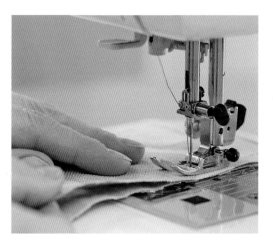

1 If necessary, join fabric and lining widths following the **Sewing a Flat Seam technique** on page 28. With right sides facing, stitch the band to one side edge of the curtain, with a 1.5 cm (⅝ in) seam allowance. Press the seam open.

2 On the right side, pin the grey gingham ribbon along the seam with the seam centred. Follow the **Applying Ribbon technique** on page 96 to stitch the ribbon in place.

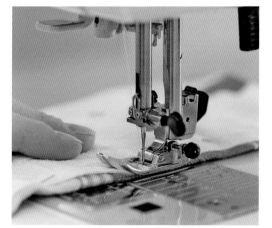

3 Follow the **Making a Lined Curtain technique** on pages 120–121 and the **Making a Curtain Heading technique** on pages 126–127 to make and line the curtain.

Curtain headings

Pencil pleat and standard curtain heading tapes are the two types of curtain heading most often used. The curtain heading is made after the curtain has been made (see pages 118–120). For an alternative style of curtain heading, see the Café Curtain project on pages 94–95.

Making a Curtain Heading

Follow these instructions for both lined and unlined curtains. If you would like the fabric to stand above a standard curtain tape heading, add double the height of the stand to the drop of the curtain in addition to the 3 cm (1¼ in) at the upper edge and the lower hem when cutting out. For example, for a 2.5 cm (1 in) stand, add 5 cm (2 in). This will give a frilled effect to the upper edge when the curtains are pulled open.

1 Press under 3 cm (1¼ in) on the upper edge of the curtain, or if the top of the curtain is to stand above the tape, press under the height of the stand plus 3 cm (1¼ in). For example, for a 2.5 cm (1 in) stand, press under 5.5 cm (2¼ in). Press the raw ends under diagonally at the corners. Knot the cords at one end of the curtain tape, then fold under the knotted end of the tape and cords.

2 Starting 5 mm (¼ in) from one side edge, pin the tape just below the upper pressed edge on the underside of the curtain, or, if the curtain is to stand above the tape, pin the tape the height of the stand below the upper edge. Continue pinning the tape to the curtain, covering the raw edges.

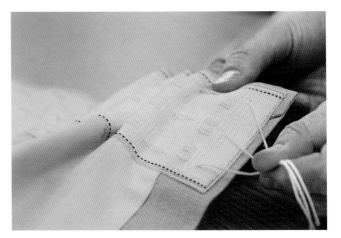

3 Cut off the excess tape 2 cm (¾ in) beyond the other edge of the curtain. Turn under 2.5 cm (1 in) at the extending end of the tape, leaving the cords on the right side—you may need to unthread the cords at the end of the tape. Stitch close to both long edges and across the turned-under ends, taking care not to catch in the extending ends of the cords. Stitch both long edges in the same direction to avoid dragging the tape in the opposite direction.

4 Pull up the cords to gather the curtain to the required width. Knot the free ends of the cords together, but don't cut them off, as you may need to open the heading out flat for laundering or hanging at a different window. Adjust the gathers evenly. Slip the hooks through the slots in the tape, placing one at each end and then at approximately 5 cm (2 in) intervals.

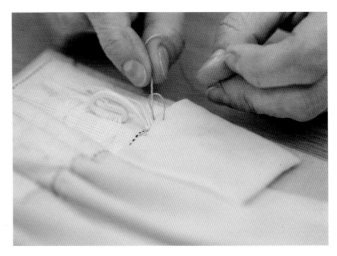

5 Roll up the excess tape and catch to the top of the curtain with a few hand stitches. Alternatively, slip the cords into a cord tidy. To make a cord tidy, cut a 15 x 7 cm (6 x 2¾ in) rectangle of fabric. With right sides facing, fold in half parallel with the short edges. Stitch the side edges, taking a 1 cm (⅜ in) seam allowance. Clip the corners and turn right side out.

6 Turn 1 cm (⅜ in) to the inside at the top of the cord tidy. Slip the cords inside the cord tidy and sew it to the top of the curtain on the underside.

YOU WILL NEED

- 112 cm (44 in) wide deep pink spotted cotton fabric (quantity depends on size of curtain)
- 112 cm (44 in) wide deep pink on white patterned cotton fabric (quantity depends on size of curtain)
- Twice the recess width plus 2 cm (¾ in) of 1.5 cm (⅝ in) wide deep pink ready-made bias binding (alternatively, make your own bias binding—see page 57)
- Twice the recess width plus 4 cm (1½ in) of 3 cm (1¼ in) wide standard curtain tape

CUTTING OUT

Measure the drop and width of the recess for the curtain.

From deep pink spotted cotton fabric, cut:

- The curtain drop plus 3.5 cm (1½ in) x twice the curtain width plus 5 cm (2 in) for side hems for the curtain

From deep pink on white patterned cotton fabric, cut:

- Four times the curtain width plus 2 cm (¾ in) for hems x 7 cm (2¾ in) for the frill

Cupboard curtain

A colourful curtain is an attractive and practical way to conceal a recess such as under a sink to hide a cluttered storage area or to enclose a cupboard while offering a softer alternative to a solid door. Add a fetching frill in a contrasting pattern to create a shabby chic look.

1 If necessary, join fabric widths following the **Sewing a Flat Felled Seam technique** on page 33. Press under 1 cm (⅜ in) and then 1.5 cm (⅝ in) on the side edges of the curtain. Stitch close to the inner pressed edges. Hem the ends and lower edge of the frill, then gather and tack the frill to the lower edge of the curtain following the **Making a Single Frill technique** on page 104. Follow the **Binding a Straight Edge technique** on page 57 to stitch the binding to the tacked seam with the right side of the binding facing the wrong side of the frill.

2 Follow the **Finishing Binding technique** on page 57, stitching close to the inner pressed edges.

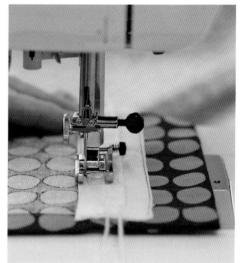

3 Follow the **Making a Curtain Heading technique** on pages 126–127, adding a 2.5 cm (1 in) stand to the top of the curtain.

Filled shapes

With this versatile technique you can create and stuff any shape of your choosing, from a dainty bird to hold potpourri to a pad for an unusually shaped cushion such as a star or a heart. The key issue to bear in mind is that you need to leave a gap for turning through the shapes once they are stitched—if possible on a straight part, as it's easier to slipstitch straight edges closed than curved ones.

Making a Filled Shape

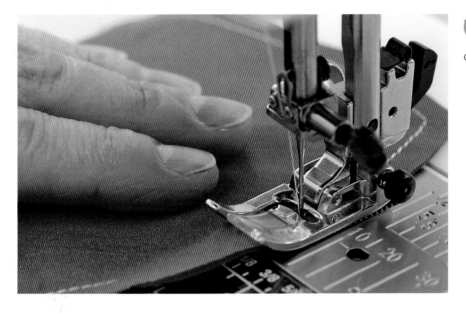

1 Stitch the shape, leaving a gap to turn right side out. Snip curves and clip corners.

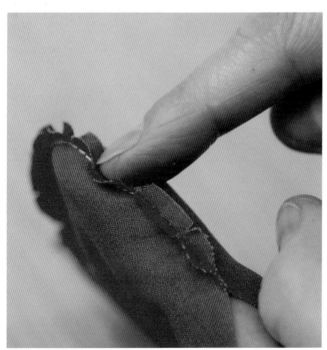

2 Finger press the seams of small shapes open by supporting the seam inside with one hand. Splay the seam open, then run a moistened finger of the other hand along the seam. Leave to dry before turning right side out. Alternatively, a sleeve board is useful for getting into narrow shapes. Press rounded seams on a tailor's ham, or improvise and fold a pad from a clean tea (dish) towel, then insert it into the shape.

Tip: You can insert a zip fastening into a star or heart-shaped cushion—just make a pattern for half the cushion and add a 1.5 cm (⅝ in) seam allowance for the zip.

3 Turn the shape to the right side. Turn corners to a point by gently easing the corner into shape with a pin. Don't overwork the corner, as the snipped seam allowance could fray and show on the right side.

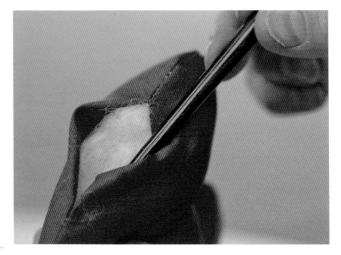

4 To stuff the shape with polyester toy filling, tease the stuffing apart before inserting it—avoid pushing in dense lumps of filling or the effect will be bumpy. To push the filling into narrow areas and points, use a rounded tool such as the end of an artist's paintbrush handle—don't use a pointed tool, as it could break the stitches.

5 You may wish to fill the shape with other fillings such as potpourri to make a potpourri sachet, polystyrene beads to make a bean bag, rice to make a doorstop or sawdust to make a pin cushion. Roll a piece of paper into a funnel and secure the shape with sticky tape. Push the narrow end of the funnel into the cavity and pour in your chosen filling. A spoon can also be used for potpourri or rice.

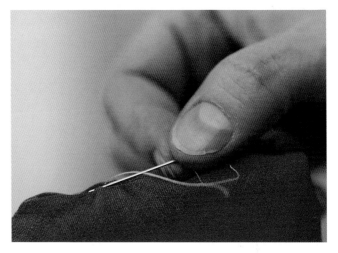

6 Pin the pressed edges of the gap closed, then slipstitch the edges together (see page 25). Keep the stitches particularly small if enclosing rice or sawdust.

YOU WILL NEED

- 10 cm (4in) square of turquoise spotted cotton fabric
- 10 cm (4in) square of iron-on medium interfacing
- 25 cm (10 in) square of pink and turquoise on white patterned cotton fabric
- Two 1 cm (3/8 in) mother-of-pearl buttons
- 20 cm (1/4 yd) of 6 mm (1/4 in) wide olive green ribbon
- 20 g (3/4 oz) dried lavender
- Two 5 mm (1/4 in) blue beads

CUTTING OUT

Press the interfacing to the wrong side of turquoise spotted cotton fabric, then refer to the template on page 141 to cut one beak and two wings

From pink and turquoise on white patterned cotton fabric:

- Refer to the template on page 141 to cut two birds

Bird potpourri sachet

Fill this charming little bird with fragrant dried lavender to scent a room. It has light-catching mother-of-pearl buttons to secure its wings in place and a pair of pretty blue beads for eyes, as well as a ribbon loop for hanging. It would make a delightful gift for a special friend.

1 Fold the beak in half along the broken lines with wrong sides facing. With the fold of the beak at the top, tack (baste) the straight edge of the beak to the right side of one bird between the dots. With right sides facing up, pin a wing to each bird. Sew a button at the dot to fix a wing to each bird.

2 Fold a 20 cm (1/4 yd) length of 6 mm (1/4 in) wide olive green ribbon in half. Tack (baste) the ribbon ends to one bird at the cross. Adjust the loop of the ribbon to lie between the dots for the gap, so that it isn't caught in the stitches when stitching the birds together.

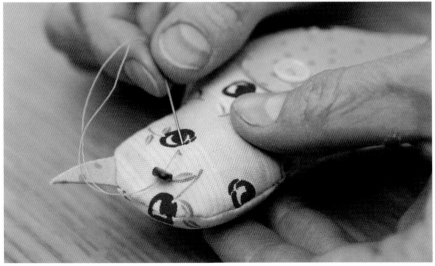

3 Following the **Making a Filled Shape technique** on pages 130–131, make the bird, taking a 6 mm (¼ in) seam allowance and filling the bird with dried lavender. Sew a blue bead to the dot on either side of the bird's head for eyes.

Tassels

Tassels can be generous and sumptuous or small and dainty. Although they are expensive to buy, they are simple to make from a variety of yarns. Stranded cotton embroidery thread (floss) is the most versatile and comes in lots of colours including metallic effects. Also consider using wool, bouclé thread and fine ribbon, or try a mixture of textures.

Making a Tassel

1 Cut a 7.5 cm (3 in) wide rectangle of card that is twice the intended length of the tassel plus 2.5 cm (1 in). Fold the card in half, parallel with the 7.5 cm (3 in) edges. Bind your chosen yarn, thread or ribbon around the card many times, depending upon the thickness of the tassel required.

2 Fold a 30 cm (12 in) length of yarn in half—if you are making the tassel from a thick yarn or fine ribbon, use a finer thread for this. Thread the ends of the yarn through the eye of a blunt-nosed needle. Slip the needle behind the strands close to the fold, then insert the needle through the loop of the yarn. This yarn will be used to suspend the tassel.

3 Holding the yarn at the folded edge of the card, slip the tips of a pair of scissors between the card layers and cut through the strands. Pull the yarn tightly to suspend the tassel. Discard the card and remove the needle.

4 Thread the needle with a single 30 cm (12 in) length of yarn. Hold the end of the yarn level with the cut ends of the tassel, then bind the yarn tightly around the head of the tassel about ten times, gathering the strands tightly together.

5 To secure, insert the needle into the bulk of the tassel above the binding. Pull the thread taut to lose the end of the yarn within the tassel, then remove the needle.

6 Cut the tassel ends level. Use the suspending yarn at the top to sew the tassel in place. To attach to a key, knot the yarns to the key, then insert the yarns threaded on a needle through the top of the tassel to lose the ends within the tassel. Cut off the excess yarn.

Tip: Beads can be sewn to the yarn binding the tassel, for an extra decorative touch.

Bound-edge napkin

Use a colourful linen for the body of this napkin and add a contrasting binding in a fabric that coordinates with your favourite tablecloth. As a finishing touch, a handmade tassel that picks up the colour of your china will give your table setting perfect cohesion.

1 To prepare the chequered bias binding, join the bias strips and make the binding, following the **Joining Bias Strips** and **Making Bias Binding techniques** on pages 56–57. Open out one folded edge of the binding and press under 5 mm (¼ in) at one end to start. With the right side of the binding facing the wrong side of the napkin and starting on one side edge of the napkin, pin the binding to the edge of the napkin, matching the raw edges. Snip the binding to the fold line at the corner, then continue pinning the binding and snipping it at each corner.

2 Stitch along the fold line. Overlap the ends of the binding and cut off the excess 1 cm (⅜ in) beyond the start of the binding. Clip the seam allowance across the corners.

3 Lift the binding out from the napkin. Press the seam towards the napkin. Press the binding to the right side on two opposite edges of the napkin. Pin the inner pressed edges to the napkin. Press the diagonal folds that form at the corners.

4 Press the adjacent edges of the binding to the right side of the napkin and pin in place. Slipstitch the diagonal edges of the binding (see page 25). Topstitch close to the inner pressed edge. Following the **Making a Tassel technique** on pages 134–135, make a 3 cm (1¼ in) long tassel from pale green stranded cotton embroidery thread (floss). Sew the tassel to one corner of the napkin.

Patterns and templates

You will need the patterns and templates printed on these pages for some of the home sewing projects in the book. Trace the patterns and templates onto tracing paper or enlarge on a photocopier where indicated. Remember to transfer any grain lines, fold lines, dots and any other useful information onto your paper pattern.

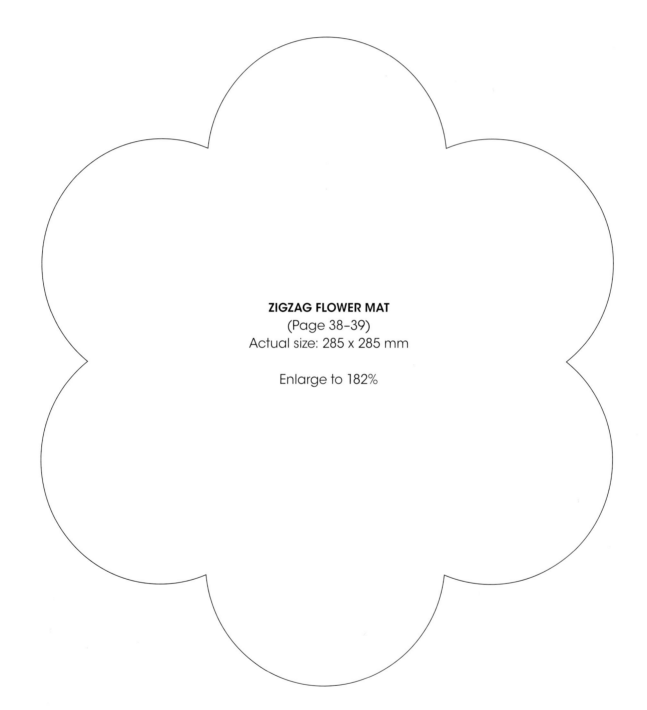

ZIGZAG FLOWER MAT
(Page 38–39)
Actual size: 285 x 285 mm

Enlarge to 182%

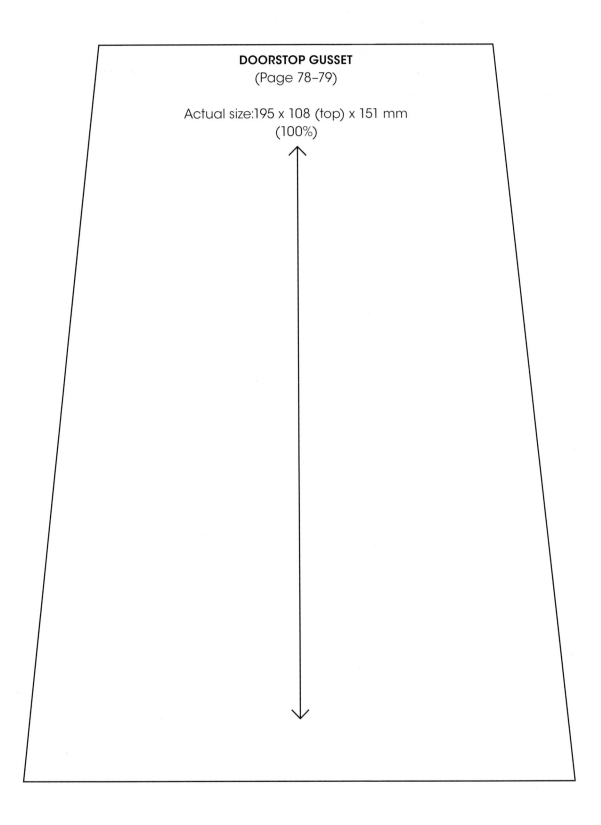

DOORSTOP GUSSET
(Page 78–79)

Actual size:195 x 108 (top) x 151 mm
(100%)

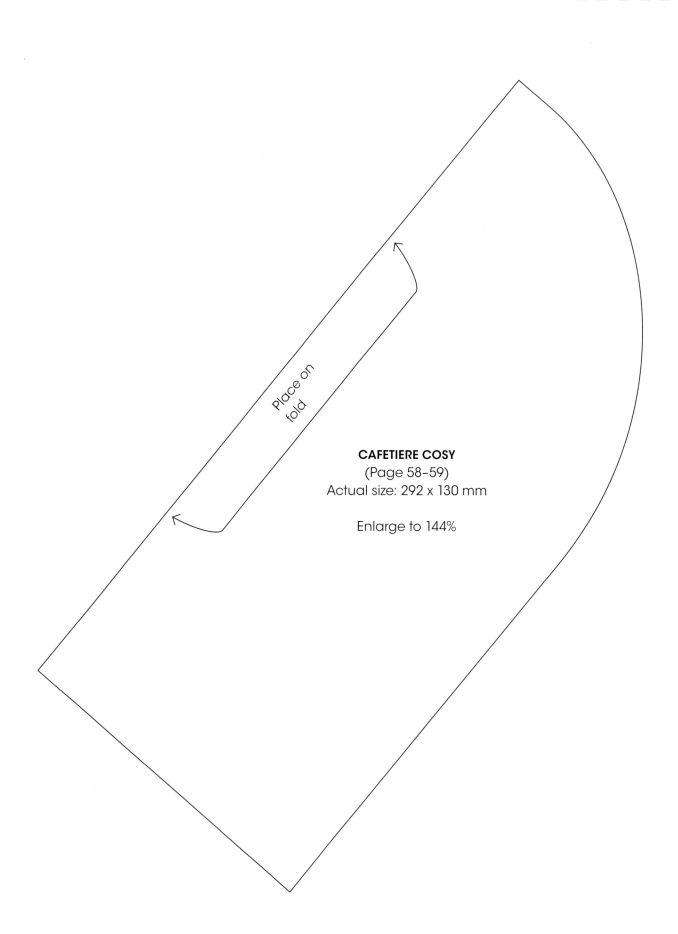

Place on fold

CAFETIERE COSY
(Page 58–59)
Actual size: 292 x 130 mm

Enlarge to 144%

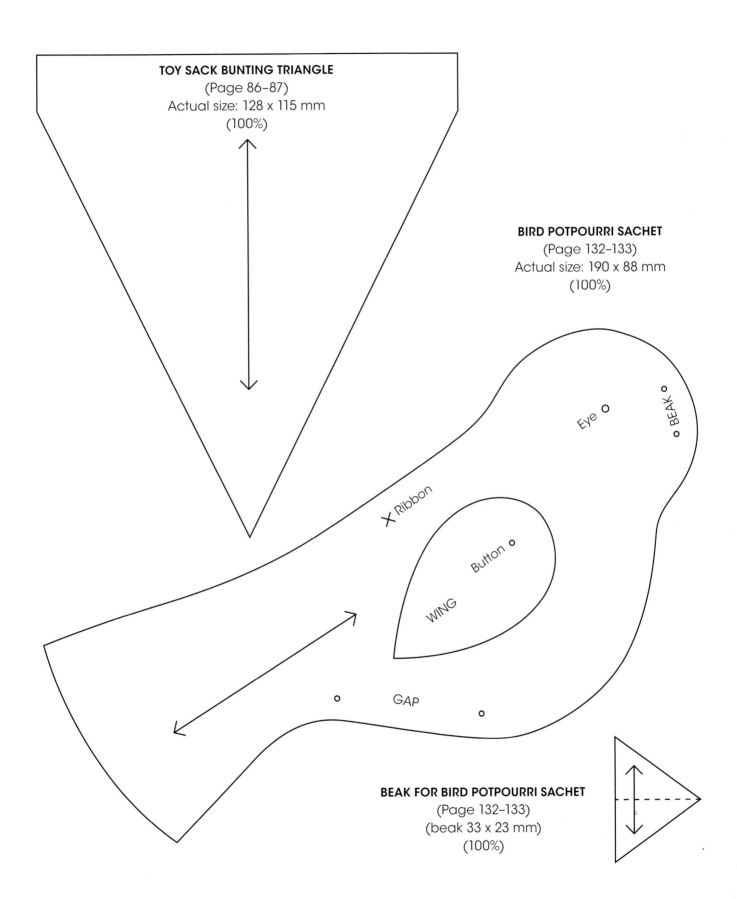

TOY SACK BUNTING TRIANGLE
(Page 86–87)
Actual size: 128 x 115 mm
(100%)

BIRD POTPOURRI SACHET
(Page 132–133)
Actual size: 190 x 88 mm
(100%)

X Ribbon

Eye ○

○ BEAK

Button ○

WING

○

GAP

○

BEAK FOR BIRD POTPOURRI SACHET
(Page 132–133)
(beak 33 x 23 mm)
(100%)

Index

Acknowledgements

Special thanks to Vanessa Arbuthnott for the beautiful soft furnishing fabric used for the Soft Cuffed Box on pages 42–43, Headboard Cover on pages 62–65, Button-fastened Cushion on pages 82–83, Chair Seat Cover on pages 110–111 and the Upholstered Footstool on pages 114–115.

See www.vanessaarbuthnott.co.uk or phone 01285 831437.